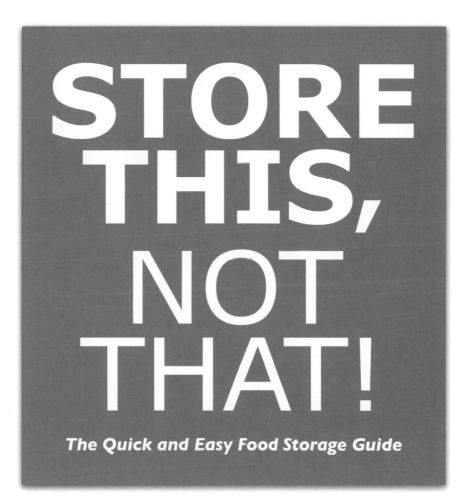

STORE THIS, NOT THAT!

The Quick and Easy Food Storage Guide

ISBN 13: 978-1-4621-1804-5

Published by Front Table Books, an imprint of Cedar Fort, Inc.
2373 W. 700 S., Springville, UT 84663
Distributed by Cedar Fort, Inc., www.cedarfort.com

LIBRARY OF CONGRESS CATALOGING-IN-PUBLICATION DATA
Godfrey, Crystal, 1983- author.
Store this, not that! / Crystal Godfrey and Debbie Kent.
    pages cm
ISBN 978-1-4621-1804-5 (acid-free paper)
1. Food--Storage. 2. Food--Preservation. 3. Canning and preserving. I. Kent, Debbie, 1958- author. II. Title.
TX601.G53 2015
641.4'8--dc23
                              2015029854

Cover and page design by M. Shaun McMurdie and Crystal Godfrey
Cover design © 2016 Lyle Mortimer
Edited by Justin Greer

Printed in the United States of America

10 9 8 7 6 5 4 3 2

Printed on acid-free paper

Savvy tips and tricks for surviving and thriving with your food storage

Learn the secrets food storage companies don't want you to know.

Store this and save more than $500 per person!

Store it to eat it! Get our full food storage menu.

Know when meal buckets are a bargain and when they aren't.

Don't make these common 72-hour kit mistakes.

BONUS!
Do-it-yourself guide to save you even more.

STORE THIS, NOT THAT!

The Quick and Easy Food Storage Guide

What you REALLY need to know about storing desserts.

Find hidden supermarket savings for stocking up.

CRYSTAL GODFREY AND DEBBIE KENT

FRONT TABLE BOOKS | AN IMPRINT OF CEDAR FORT, INC. | SPRINGVILLE, UTAH

This book is dedicated to all those who find the world of food storage
to be complex and even a little scary. May this book be an essential tool
for safeguarding your family against the storms of life.

Also, to our wonderful and brave families, who are our number-one fans.
We love you! Thank you for your listening ears, your continual support, and
especially your willingness to taste-test recipes and products—even those
that were so bad the dog wouldn't eat them.

contents

Introduction

Hi, friends!

We love food storage and the feeling of security it brings. Let us empower you with the secrets of successful food storage.
—Crystal & Debbie

Let's face it, food storage can be confusing, frustrating, and downright daunting. If you've ever felt confused about what you should actually be buying and storing, you're not alone—and we're here to help! We help people all over the United States decipher this crazy world of food storage, and we can do it for YOU! We promise this book will be simple and straightforward, and in just a few hours it will teach you everything you need to know to be your own food storage pro.

YOU DESERVE THE PEACE OF PREPAREDNESS

Somewhere, somehow, over the last few years, something happened to the economy and the world. We all know it. We've felt the effects of it, and let's be honest, it's got everyone pretty concerned.

LET'S BREAK IT DOWN FOR YOU:

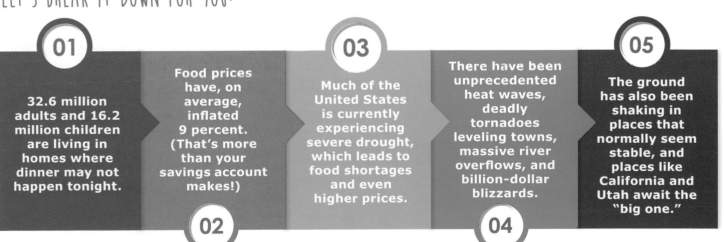

01 32.6 million adults and 16.2 million children are living in homes where dinner may not happen tonight.

02 Food prices have, on average, inflated 9 percent. (That's more than your savings account makes!)

03 Much of the United States is currently experiencing severe drought, which leads to food shortages and even higher prices.

04 There have been unprecedented heat waves, deadly tornadoes leveling towns, massive river overflows, and billion-dollar blizzards.

05 The ground has also been shaking in places that normally seem stable, and places like California and Utah await the "big one."

Couple that with a struggling economy and with rising food and gas prices and you have a real problem. The point of these facts and figures is not to depress or scare you. It's to reassure you that if you don't have all the food storage you want or need, this is a cause worth fighting, scrimping, sacrificing, and saving for. It's to reassure you that you have made the right choice to be prepared! In fact, we think you and your family deserve it! You deserve the peace preparedness brings, the comfort of knowing you have food for your family, and the tools you'll need to make a preemptive strike on rising food prices. It's never too late to begin or finish what you have started—and that is where we come in . . .

BETWEEN FRIENDS

If you know us, you know we have a fun, lighthearted, no-nonsense approach to food storage. We've been successful at helping people get motivated to actually obtain and use their food storage. We decided to write this book because after all our classes, TV appearances, seminars, and speeches, people still ask us, "What's the secret to getting your food storage?" Even our own friends ask us this. They say things like "We don't have time to learn everything we need to know, read a long book, or take a class. Just tell me what to do—can't you just do it for me? What's the secret?"

And since we're all friends now, we'll let you in on all of our secrets and show you how we can do it all for you! Between us we've been in the food storage business for over 18 years and have worked with or for most of the big food storage companies—which makes us the perfect team to give you the inside scoop on the best available products.

Crystal is the author of the popular food storage book *I Can't Believe It's Food Storage* and is a food storage blogger, where her job is to test out the latest food storage products, discover new ways to use them, and compile the newest, smartest, most authoritative information on food storage available. She has had several television appearances on Salt Lake's *Studio 5* and BYUtv and has taught many people how to simplify cooking with food storage.

Debbie has been involved in food storage since she was a teen. For the past 14 years she has taught cooking with food storage and preparedness seminars in southern California, Idaho, and across Utah, where she shares her knowledge of the good, the bad, and the sometimes funny truths in the world of preparedness and delights her audiences with her easygoing and enthusiastic "can-do" approach.

Follow us on Pinterest

Find our favorite food storage recipes and emergency preparedness ideas.
pinterest.com/stntfoodstorage

STORE THIS NOT THAT
IT'S NOT JUST FOR WHEN THE WORLD ENDS.

MONTHLY CLASSES
Save the date

Join us every month for our classes on food storage and emergency preparedness!

More information at
www.storethisnotthat.com

That is why we're so excited about this book! You deserve to be able to make the best choices for your family—you are the only one that can do that. You need to be empowered with unbiased information in food storage options from REAL experts. It can tangle your brain to decide if you should store canned chicken versus freeze-dried or if it's really worth it to have freeze-dried ice cream sandwiches on hand for when everything hits the fan and your family is screaming for ice cream. We'll give you all the information you need to know if you should be storing this, not that.

So let's get started! We'll coach you through every step of successfully obtaining your food storage. In just a few hours, we believe you'll be surprised by how much your thinking can change. And as your thinking changes, you'll begin to see—as thousands of people already have—that you can have the peace of preparedness and provide for your family, no matter what!

CONNECT WITH US!

ASK US A QUESTION! storethisnotthat@gmail.com

FACEBOOK *facebook.com/storethisnotthat*

INSTAGRAM *instagram.com/storethisnotthat*

PINTEREST *pinterest.com/stntfoodstorage*

HOW THIS BOOK WILL HELP YOU SAVE $ EAT BETTER

and never go hungry again!

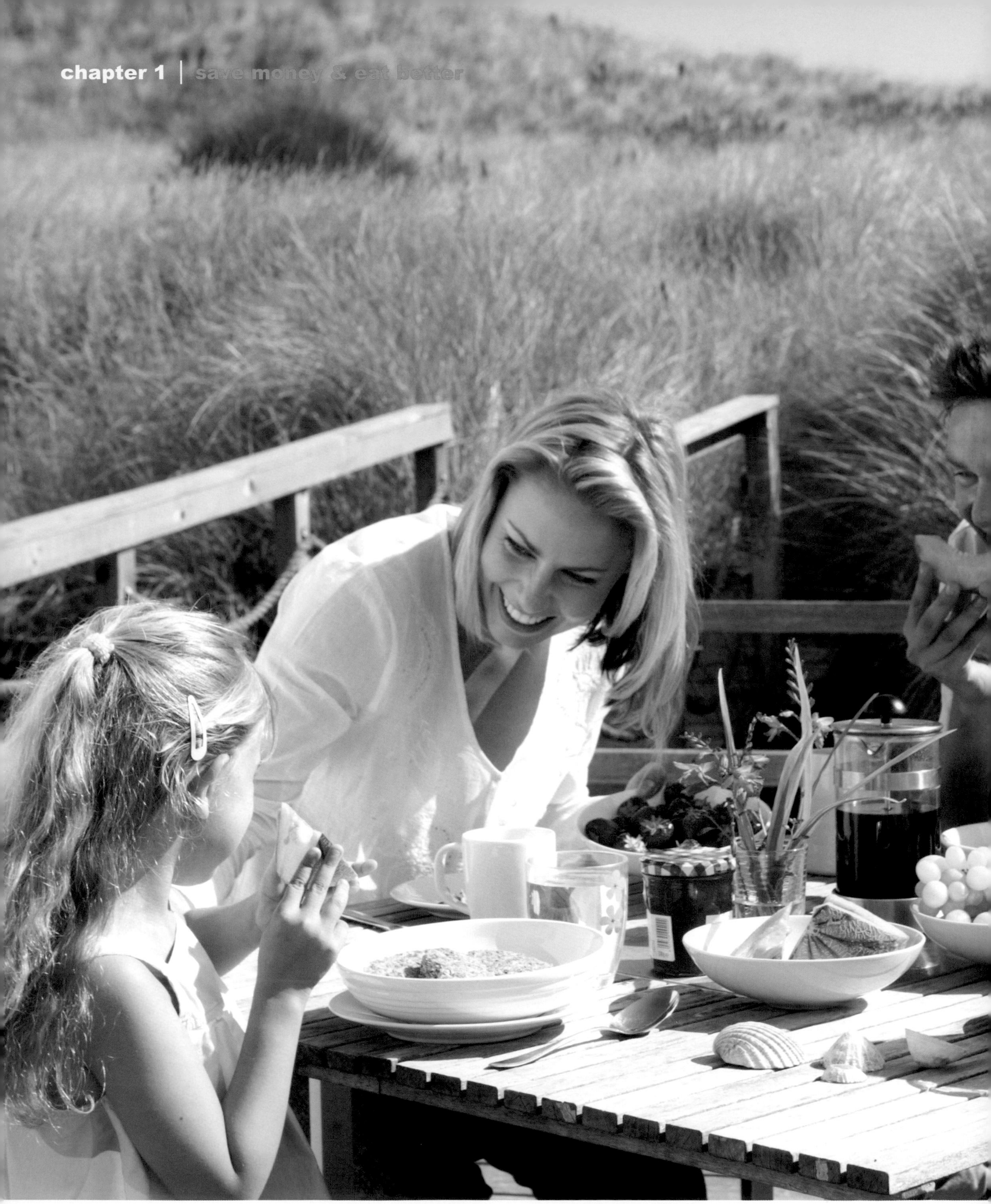

Here's the dirty little secret the food storage industry doesn't want you to know:

FOOD STORAGE IS MUCH EASIER AND CHEAPER THAN YOU THINK!

We know, we know: if you've seen the guys donned in camo gear waving a gun around while canning wheat, visited a food storage store, sat through a boring class, listened to your grandmother, or attended a party full of lame games and food storage samples, then you've received a bunch of different messages about what your family should have as its food storage. Some tell you only freeze-dried food, or that it's only for when the world ends, or that storing enough MREs to feed a village is the easiest way to go.

While preparedness is great in any form, food storage primarily is a matter of knowing what to store and how to turn it into meals your family would actually eat. And, theoretically, that ought to be easy. So what's with all the craziness? Why are 95% of Americans not prepared? Why do so many people have nightmares about actually needing to eat their food storage? Why are so many people spending outrageous amounts on the food they are storing (like spending $10,000 for a three-month supply of food!)? It's because no one looks at food storage as regular food, in terms of cost or use. That is why this book is truly revolutionary. It offers real answers to questions of what to store and what not to store.

The Real
WAY TO STORE FOOD

When it comes time to assess the most popular food storage items, don't just look at the cute labels. Take a deeper dive into the cost, health benefits, storability, and usability. Keep in mind that foods with seemingly unbelievable storage claims often don't live up to their promises.

FOOD STORAGE DEEP DARK SECRET #1: EMERGENCY FOOD BUCKETS

Think about this phrase: "Emergency Food Bucket." We've all been tempted at the possibility of purchasing a cheap bucket of food that promises to be everything we would need during an emergency. But is it really? In 2006, Costco was sued because they claimed the food was a 3-month supply of food for one person, yet the caloric intake was just 455 calories per day. The average adult should consume roughly 2,000 calories per day. Unfortunately, even those claiming to be 2,000 calories are usually filled with empty sugar drink calories or meals full of mashed potatoes and rice. So how is anyone to know when or if these buckets are ever a good idea to buy? (Hint: We do!)

FOOD STORAGE DEEP DARK SECRET #2: FREEZE-DRIED FOOD

Consider all the hype about freeze-dried foods. You know, how freeze-dried fruits and vegetables are more nutritious than their dehydrated or canned counterparts. But did you know that according to a study done by the University of Illinois, canned fruits and vegetables provide as much dietary fiber and vitamins as the same corresponding fresh foods, and in some cases, even more? And with the price of freeze-dried foods up to 10 times the price of canned, it's important to know which freeze-dried foods will give you the biggest bang for your buck—and which won't!

FOOD STORAGE DEEP DARK SECRET #3: POWDERED MILK

What about milk? Everybody knows that milk is an essential part of any diet, offering numerous health benefits. But you're drinking something more than just milk if you're drinking a "Milk Alternative Drink" with your breakfast. The technical list of ingredients is this: sweet whey, creamer (coconut oil, corn syrup solids, sodium caseinate [a milk derivative], dipotassium phosphate, sugar, mono- and diglycerides, polysorbate 80, sodium silicoaluminate, tetrasodium pyrophosphate, soy lecithin), nonfat milk, sugar, guar gum, vitamin A, and vitamin D. Yeesh! Definitely not the same ingredients listed for real powdered milk, which is simply non-fat milk and vitamin D. This popular milk alternative should not appear as a frequent guest in your food storage lineup.

If that all sounds a bit complicated . . . well, it is. Which is why we've done all the work for you. Not just showing you the "store this, not that" of food storage, but also how normal food storage meals can be. We're not talking about lentil meatloaf or clumpy powdered milk here. We're going to show you how to eat all your favorite foods—and we mean bread and dairy, burritos and macaroni and cheese, ice cream and cookies—and all with your food storage.

And it's going to be much easier than you thought!

Nutrition Facts
Serving Size: 1 Cup (30g)
Servings Per Package: About 6

Calories	110	150
Calories from Fat	10	10
		% Daily Value
Total Fat 1.5g	2%	2%
Saturated Fat 0g	0%	0%
Trans Fat 0g		
Polyunsaturated Fat 0.5g		
Monounsaturated Fat 0.5g		
Cholesterol 0mg	0%	1%
Sodium 210mg	9%	11%
Total Carbohydrate 24g	8%	10%
Dietary Fiber 2g	8%	8%
Sugars 10g		
Protein 2g		

Vitamin A	10%	15%
Vitamin C	10%	10%
Calcium	10%	25%
Iron	50%	50%
Vitamin D	10%	25%
Thiamin	25%	30%
Riboflavin	25%	35%
Niacin	25%	25%
Vitamin B6	25%	25%
Folate (Folic Acid)	50%	50%
Vitamin B12	10%	20%
Phosphorus	25%	35%
Zinc	25%	30%

Your Simple

AND EFFECTIVE FOOD STORAGE GUIDE

To help you navigate this food storage maze, we'll be explaining which foods you should be storing and which you shouldn't. It's simple; we've created easy-to-decipher charts, stunningly blunt "Store This, Not That!" recommendations, and information you never knew. We'll explain the evidence that demonstrates the nutritional value, cost per serving, and usability, so you can make the right choices and be more prepared than you knew possible. We'll also show you how to avoid the common mistakes that can undermine your food storage preparations.

From now on, you're never going to have to wonder about what food storage to buy or how to use it. We've done the research for you. We've compared thousands of food storage items, checked each category to make sure that you get the most for your money, considered the health benefits, and organized it in a way that's easy to understand and without any of the ridiculous claims that are meant to mislead and confuse you. With this simple guide, you'll learn how to . . .

STORE THIS, NOT THAT! TO SAVE MONEY

We love saving money; how about you? That's why it's great to know that if you make the switch to making bread at home (it's much easier than you think and much better tasting—we promise!) it could save you $8 a week or up to $416 a year with this swap alone. Or let's say you make your own delicious and healthy granola cereal instead of buying those expensive sugar-laced cereals from the store. You'd save $6 a week, saving you $312 a year. Or if you're feeling really brave, you can replace one meal a week with a meal made with beans and rice (hey—Dave Ramsey agrees with us!) and you could save over $520 a year! That's more than $1,250 dollars a year if you choose to do all three, and we've only scratched the surface.

But wait—there's more! With *Store This, Not That!* you will also make better decisions about which food storage products to buy with your money. You won't make the mistake of buying that can of brownie mix because you'll know that it's like buying a box of brownies for $7. (And no one in their right mind would do that.) You'll also know that if you buy non-instant powdered milk instead of instant milk you could save $665. You'll also know that buying freeze-dried isn't cost effective to use every day because you're paying over $10 a pound for that meat.

STORE THIS, NOT THAT! TO EAT BETTER

If you've been thinking about eating better—and by better we mean healthier and tastier meals—you've come to the right place. Did you know that when you are cooking at home with food storage, you save money and calories? Plus, you gain control over your ingredients. The fact is, almost none of us have any idea what's really going into our food. Bigwig corporate food companies have made a science out of making their food addicting and you hungrier with every bite. Additives and preservatives derived from duck feathers, petroleum products, wood chips, and even human hair make our food what it is today. Yummy, right? When you cook at home you can take out the MSG, high fructose corn syrup, fat, food dyes, and every other impure ingredient and instead add in whole grains, more protein and fiber, and REAL ingredients.

Food storage staples such as whole grains and beans have numerous health benefits. Benefits like reducing your chance of heart disease, keeping you full longer, reducing tooth decay and gum disease, reducing your risk of colon cancer, helping you fight against type 2 diabetes, reducing your stress levels, helping you lower cholesterol levels, and most importantly, adding a lot of fiber, minerals, and vitamins to your diet.

STORE THIS, NOT THAT! TO NEVER GO HUNGRY AGAIN!

When you combine a well-planned food supply with practical skills, you are prepared for any situation. In fact, we've both had times when we were living off our food storage and garden. It was a life saver! Preparing for your family in a time of need isn't wacky, it's brilliant. Knowing you can feed and provide for your family is one of the greatest feelings of peace you will ever have.

An almost-forgotten means of economic self-reliance is the home production and storage of food. In this day and age, we are far too accustomed to taking multiple trips to the store and purchasing what we need. By producing some of our food, we reduce to a great extent the impact of inflation on our money and our ability to eat some of our favorite foods when circumstances go awry.

Take, for example, the worst bird flu outbreak to ever hit the United States, which occurred in 2015. Dubbed the poultry apocalypse, this outbreak caused the death of over 38 million chickens and turkeys and sent egg prices through the roof. If you had your food storage stocked with the correct egg product, you could still enjoy your favorite baked goods, omelets, and egg breakfasts without falling prey to the $4- or $5-a-dozen egg prices at the store.

LET'S DO THIS THING!

The food storage items have been studied, the nutrition labels analyzed, and the latest research checked and collated. On the following pages, you're going to discover the simplest, easiest food storage guide ever created!

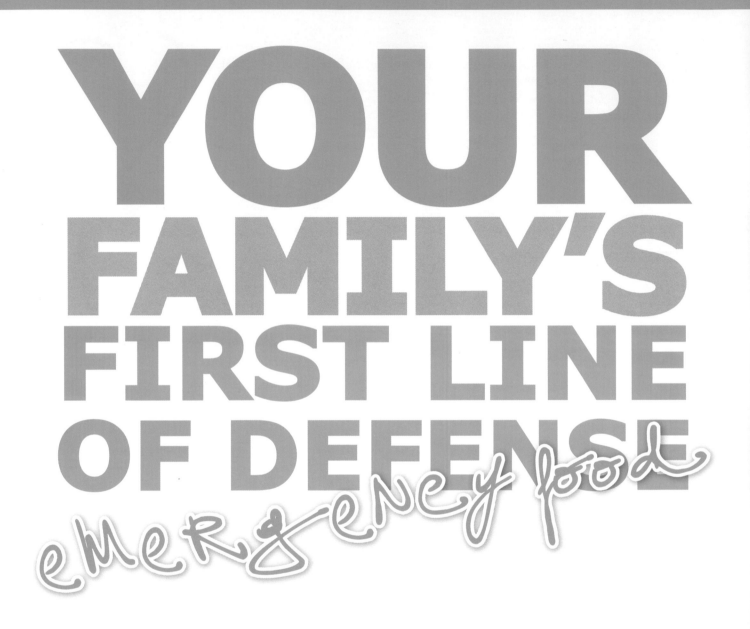

"Any state, any community, or for that matter, any citizen that fails to prepare, assuming the federal government can take care of them, will be tragically wrong."

MIKE O. LEAVITT, FORMER SECRETARY OF HEALTH AND HUMAN SERVICES

your family's first line of defense

Are you ready for this? We're about to set you leaps and bounds ahead of the vast majority of people living in the United States.

Catastrophic events such as natural and man-made disasters can happen at any moment, and most happen with NO warning. Unfortunately, 85% of the people in the United States aren't prepared to care for themselves after a disaster because they believe FEMA (the Federal Emergency Management Agency) will be there to take care of them. (Laughable, right?) History has shown us that this just isn't the case. The fact is, 91% of Americans live in places at a moderate-to-high risk of natural and man-made disasters. Most people aren't prepared, but with our help, this won't be you.

The reality is that it's a question of when, not if you will be affected. It is also a fact that you are your family's first line of defense after a disaster—not FEMA or any other agency. So if having a supply of emergency food and water is that important and vital, why don't more people prepare?

TOP REASONS WHY PEOPLE DON'T PREPARE

It won't happen.

If it does happen, it won't happen to me.

If it does happen to me, it won't be that bad.

If it happens to me and it's bad, there's always FEMA.

REASON #1   REASON #2   REASON #3   REASON #4

None of us knows when a life-changing catastrophe will strike. But fear not! There is still time to get your house in order. How do we know this? Because if there weren't, you wouldn't be reading this—but neither is there time to waste. Tomorrow could be that "very bad day," which means the best time to start is NOW!

When you are prepared, you won't worry anymore. Instead of panic, hunger, and fear, you will stay calm, have a clear head, and a clear plan of action. Having emergency food and water is your first level of preparedness. It is cheap and easy to store and will fill the void in your stomach, giving you needed energy to help yourselves and others.

SO . . . WHAT WILL IT BE LIKE?

We're so glad you asked! One of our most frequently asked questions is, "What it will really be like when a severe disaster strikes?" Honestly, this is a very important question, because when you understand what it will truly be like you can prepare much better. During an emergency situation you will be finding family, recovering belongings, assessing damage, taking care of injuries, helping friends and neighbors, etc. Life as you normally live it will be replaced with a more primitive lifestyle—one of stress, simplicity, and service. You won't be shopping or going out to dinner because the store shelves will be empty and the restaurants will be closed. You will not have the time or energy to cook. This will be the time for emergency food and water. When a severe disaster strikes your area (and it will), one of two things happen:

"If an earthquake, hurricane, winter storm, or other disaster strikes your community, you might not have access to food, water, and electricity for days or even weeks." –FEMA Website

SCENARIO #1: YOU NEED TO EVACUATE

This means you may have to leave immediately, possibly on foot, taking just what you can grab on your way out the door. Your 72-hour kit, AKA grab-and-go bag, will contain things like a change of clothes, hygiene and first aid supplies, and a flashlight. It shouldn't contain a three-course meal or a stove and dishes. You don't want that precious space and poundage in your backpack being used up by cans of food! (Which is why we aren't fans of canned tuna or chili in your 72-hour kit.)

SCENARIO #2: SHELTERING AT HOME

If it is safe to stay in your home, you will still be in shock as your whole world is turned upside-down. You may be dealing with no electricity or gas (so you may be piping hot or freezing cold depending on the season and your location), and you'll be busy helping to clean up the destruction, which includes digging through and cleaning up the debris, rescuing the trapped, and treating injuries. You'll need easy meals that don't require heat for eating because you'll be BUSY helping others around you and you may have no traditional ways of heating it.

👍 STORE THIS IN YOUR 72-HOUR KIT

CRYSTAL'S FAVORITE!

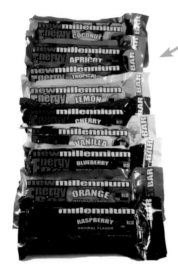

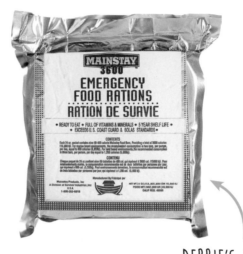

DEBBIE'S FAVORITE!

MILLENNIUM SURVIVAL BAR

Most Flavors & Variety

Price for a 3-day stash: $13
Carbs: 52g, Fiber: 1g, Protein: 8g, Vitamins: low

With 9 fruity flavors, you're sure to find the right one for you! Plus, you can have multiple flavors in your pack.

MAINSTAY SURVIVAL BAR

Great Value & Taste

Price for a 3-day stash: $8
Carbs: 46g, Fiber: 2g, Protein: 3g, Vitamins: high

This almost tastes like your grandmother's shortbread with a slightly sweet and lemony flavor.

DATREX SURVIVAL BAR

Good Value

Price for a 3-day stash: $8
Carbs: 42g, Fiber: 0g, Protein: 6g, Vitamins: low

Datrex comes individually packaged with a slight coconut flavor. They can be a little crumbly.

HAVE A TASTE-TESTING PARTY!

Buy one of each of the kinds of bars and get together with family or friends and have a tasting party. You may find, as we did, that while you may think a particular kind of bar tastes absolutely disgusting, your spouse may love it. One of the greatest things about survival bars is that they are sold individually so everyone in the family can have the flavor that they love!

You'll want food that is quick and easy to eat but gives you energy, doesn't require water or cooking, stores for a long time (5+ years), and can be stored at varying temperatures, including extreme heat and cold. As an added bonus, it should taste good (so you and your kids will want to eat it). Realistically, when you are under a lot of emotional stress the last thing your body wants is a big meal to digest. Your main reason for eating will be energy and survival. The perfect solution to this dilemma is survival bars. They are compact (about the size of a paperback novel), weigh under 2 pounds, provide energy, protein, and vitamins, and are made for eating on the go. They are also non–thirst provoking, safely store at very low and very high temperatures, have a 5-year shelf life, cost around $10 for a three-day supply, and provide 1200 calories per day.

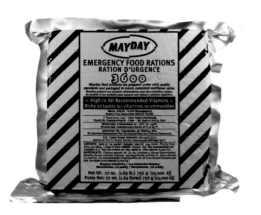

MAYDAY SURVIVAL BAR

High in Carbs & Protein

Price for a 3-day stash: $10
Carbs: 55g, Fiber: 2g, Protein: 7g, Vitamins: high

These come in lightly scored bars (be prepared with a way to cut them) with a light cinnamon-apple flavor.

ER SURVIVAL BAR

High in Carbs & Protein

Price for a 3-day stash: $10
Carbs: 52g, Fiber: 2g, Protein: 7g, Vitamins: medium

ER bars have a vanilla flavor but can be very dry and break apart easily.

SOS SURVIVAL BAR

Good Value & High in Protein

Price for a 3-day stash: $8
Carbs: 53g, Fiber: 0g, Protein: 8g, Vitamins: low

SOS bars are individually wrapped and have a slight coconut flavor.

got allergies?

We have the perfect survival bar for you! *The Original Survival Bar* is a vegan and gluten-free survival bar that comes in 6 flavors. High in fiber and protein (possible side effects), low in vitamins. Stores 6 months at a cool temperature (so plan on rotating them). Do not store in car. Costs $33 for a 3-day stash

NOT THAT
IN YOUR
72-HOUR KIT

GRANOLA BARS
Bulky

Granola bars go rancid (especially in hot temperatures) in only 6 months. Plus, at only 100 calories per bar, you'd have to pack 36 bars to equal the calories and nutrition of the survival bar.

ENERGY BARS
Expensive!

Energy bars also have a short shelf life and can be a mess in hot temperatures. You'd have to store about 30 energy bars to equal the calories of the survival bar, and at an average price of $2 a bar, that is expensive!

CANNED FOOD
Bad, Bad, Bad

Canned foods are bulky and heavy and need a can opener to open them. Oh, you think pop top lids are a great idea? They pop open when pressure is applied, and sometimes they just pop open for the heck of it, leaving a yucky mess and no food to eat.

36 bars = 1 package survival bar

$60 for a 3-day supply that has to be rotated every 6 months!

Cans add up to an extra 9 pounds to your pack!

There are many "cute" ideas floating out there in cyberspace for 72-hour kit food. Most of them, while they have good intentions, are not the best choice for high-stress, low-water situations. We are sure you have seen some of them. They seem to revolve around three main ideas. 1) Stuff as many thirst-provoking snacks into a gallon jug or bag as possible; 2) fill your bag full of canned foods that are heavy, bulky, and unappetizing (such as the tuna and applesauce combo); or 3) carry foods that are dry, need water added (8+ pounds per gallon), and have to be cooked, meaning fuel, pan, utensils, and time. We understand the need for familiar foods, and you can have all you want in your two-week emergency food supply (next page). It's really best to keep your 72-hour kit food light, compact, and as easy to eat as possible. If you need some comfort food, throw in some hard candy and gum. The following make our NOT THAT list.

HOMEMADE SURVIVAL BAR
Big and Bulky

Makes 3 very hard, jello-flavored bulky bricks. Bars made from oats, powdered milk, and sugar, with claims of 2,000 calories each. Nutritional content and indefinite storage life are unverified.
Cost: $11

MRE
High Salt, Low Fiber

MREs, or Meals Ready to Eat, are complete meals made for soldiers on the go. They will make you very thirsty and constipated, not a good position be in when water is in short supply and the potty's not working.

SLIM JIM
Unappetizing

Besides the fact that these are very greasy and high in salt, they might be difficult to stomach when you are walking through streets of destruction and death. If you "need" some meat to chew on, use jerky as a replacement—still high in salt but no grease.

These popular claims are untested . . . is it a gamble you're willing to take?

MREs are meant to stop you up . . . if you catch our drift.

Greasy foods may leave your stomach queasy.

HEAT & EAT MEALS

THE NEXT TWO WEEKS

Heat & Eat foods are important to fill your belly and provide energy as you work your way through the physical and mental stresses that will surround you during the next few weeks. These can be any foods that are shelf stable and fall into the "open; add water (if necessary); heat and eat" category. These types of food can be eaten cold, right out of the can or box if necessary, and require very little energy or brain power to make. They make it easy to conserve your water and fuel for more important things, all while refueling your body and soul to give you that little extra to cope with the chaos around you. People feel and deal with life better when they have eaten one filling meal per day with family or friends.

CANNED AND PREPACKAGED MEALS

Heat & Eat foods include canned and pre-packaged meals, but don't just run out to the store and grab any ol' canned food from off the shelf. You will want these to be things that your family likes to eat because eating familiar foods provides comfort in times of stress. Try to include foods that are high in calories, carbs, and protein. Most canned and boxed foods can safely be stored for 2–5 years.

Examples of these are soup, chili, stew, ravioli, fruits, cup o' noodles, canned chicken salad and crackers, dry soup mixes, complete meals in a box, oatmeal, and cereal. Don't forget the snacks, including granola bars and maybe even some chocolate, but these need to be rotated every 6 months!

👍 STORE THIS!

FREEZE-DRIED MEALS

If you want to include freeze-dried meals in your food storage, this is the place for them. They store for 20+ years (if stored in a cool place), and you just need to add water, heat, and eat. They come in a variety of flavors, and include breakfasts, main dishes, and even desserts.

A word of caution . . . you will need to store extra water—about double the daily gallon per person. Do not eat them dry because they need moisture to rehydrate and will absorb any available moisture in your body during digestion, causing mild to severe pain and distress, probably not what you want to be dealing with during an already stressful time. Hint: make sure to try these out ahead of time and store varieties your family likes.

30-DAY EMERGENCY FOOD BUCKET

Those "30 days of emergency food in a bucket" seem to be popping up everywhere these days. If you are thinking about purchasing one, think again. Don't be fooled by their claims of a month's worth of delicious food, all for a great low price. They are gimmicks, pure and simple.

If you take the time to read the small print you will find out most of their claims of 300+ servings usually include

- Extremely small portion sizes, such as ¼ cup juice or milk and ½-cup meals.
- Low daily calories, in the 500–1200 calorie range (we need more, not less, when we are stressed).
- Little variety: 2–3 breakfasts, 4–5 main meals. Some meals are only mashed potatoes or rice.
- Meals packaged to make 4–5 servings at a time, not the one person that the bucket is designed for.
- Very little protein, fiber, and carbohydrates.

All in all, these are not a good choice for filling the belly, keeping strong, or comforting the soul during stressful times. If you really feel the need to store these, be sure to supplement them with meat and bread, and don't forget to store lots of extra water!

👎 NOT THAT!

MEALS READY TO EAT (MRE)

MREs made our list again! We don't recommend MREs (Meals Ready to Eat) for a variety of reasons. These are food packs that are designed and packaged for the military. To get their full nutritional value, you need to eat all parts of the kit, the main meal, the crackers and spread, etc. All are very high in fats and salt—LOTS of salt and VERY low in fiber. They also do NOT store well in the heat or cold. Most people think they have a five-year shelf life, but in reality it is closer to three, and if exposed to high heat, like in your car trunk, it can drop to as little as three months. In addition, they aren't cheap; with shipping they cost over $6 per meal. Lastly, they don't taste all that great. You can do a lot better than MREs.

TRY THIS!

MAKE YOUR OWN MEALS

A great way to save money and customize your meals is to put together your own homemade meals and mixes. These can include meals in a bag or bottle that you put together yourself. There are lots of books out there to get you started. Some of our favorites are: *100-Day Pantry* by Jan Jackson; *Dinner Is in the Jar* by Kathy Clark; and *Gifts in a Jar* or *It's in the Bag* by Trent and Michelle Snow. There are also many mix recipes and cookbooks to be found.

got food?
NEED WATER!

(rotate quarterly)

FOR YOUR 72-HOUR KIT

When "it" happens, it most likely will affect your ability to get clean water out of your faucet. So what will you do? You won't be buying it from the store; water sells out first thing. What about your 72-hour kit? Great idea, but did you know that most pre-assembled 72-hour kits only contain three cups of water? That's 3 cups for 3 days, which is not even enough water for a puppy!

👍 STORE THIS!

Water is heavy, weighing over 8 pounds per gallon! The suggested one gallon per day would weigh over 25 pounds and pretty much fill up your backpack. So what do you really need? 2 quarts of water and a filter to clean some more along the way. This breaks down to four 16-ounce bottles or 16 mylar bags of water.

(rotate every 5 years)

OUR FAVORITE WATER BOTTLE FILTER!

Berkey Water Filter Bottle, $17

Water bottle filters are a valuable addition to your 72-hour kits. They are lightweight and increase your capacity of safe drinking water by being able to filter questionable water sources. All you do is fill, squeeze, and sip through the filter straw for clean, great-tasting water. If the water is really dirty, pour through a bandana first to increase life of the filter.

NOT THAT! 👎

Water boxes break open if squished in your bag, and it's difficult to drink every last drop.

FOR YOUR 2-WEEK SUPPLY WHEN SHELTERING AT HOME

Remember that two weeks of emergency food you have stored? You are going to need some water to go with that too. If you want to eat, you have to drink; that is a basic rule of survival. So, in addition to your 72-hour kit water, you need to store 14 gallons of emergency water for each person. If you live in a hot area with no natural water sources and little rain, or you are planning on washing clothes or bodies at some point, it would be safer to increase this amount to 25 gallons or more per person. More is better where water is concerned.

STORE THIS! 👍

Your water supply can be stored in clean juice or soda bottles, cases of water bottles, five-gallon jugs, or 55-gallon drums (one 55-gallon drum is enough for 2–4 people). That is all there is to it, a few bottles, a case, or a jug at a time.

👎 NOT THAT

Don't store water in milk or water jugs; they leak and can be unsanitary! Water stored in bleach bottles is not safe for drinking water either. Water bricks are very expensive; $6–$12 per gallon. Your goal is to pay $1 per gallon for your water storage containers.

Be sure to get all of the needed spickets and spouts to make pouring water easy!

cooking
when the
power is out!

Some people don't mind eating cold canned food, but we like our cans of chili warmed up without chunks of grease. If you are more like us, you will want at least two ways to heat up your food and water when the power is out, and fuel to use them for 2 hours a day for 2–4 weeks. Why two ways? Because one cooker might fail or be destroyed by a catastrophe. It is also good idea to have at least one cooker that can use charcoal because charcoal is cheap, stores forever, and is easy to regulate cooking temperature. The good news is that most of you already have ways you can do this by using your barbecue, camping stove, or Dutch oven. We love these multitaskers because you can use them right now and when "it" happens! Whether it's a summer day perfect for grilling or going on a picnic or a weekend camping trip, there is no reason why these should sit around not being used. The big question is: do you have enough fuel stored to use them when the power is out? Here are some guidelines for how much fuel you will need for your two weeks of emergency cooking.

Use Kingsford Original brand charcoal (not match light) for best results. Great sales at Home Depot on Memorial Day, 4th of July, and Labor Day.

KIND OF FUEL	BURN TIME	AMOUNT FOR 2 WEEKS	FUEL COST FOR 2 WEEKS	FUEL STORAGE LIFE
Butane Bottle*	1.5 hours	14 bottles	$28	8 years
Charcoal	2 hours	4 pounds	$20	indefinitely, if dry
Coleman fuel or unleaded gas	7 days	2 gallons	$10–$20	2 years or 5 years w/ additive
Propane: 1-lb. bottle	5 hours	7 tanks	$27	indefinitely
Propane: 20-lb. tank	36 hours	1 tank	$44	indefinitely

*Only fuel that can be safely used indoors. Does not work well in temperatures below 30°.

Don't forget the wooden matches, stored in an airtight container!

WHICH COOKER IS RIGHT for you?

We often are asked, "If you could pick one cooker, which would it be?" As you will see on the following pages, there are many powerless cookers to choose from. Generally, we really like the All-American Sun Oven and the Volcano Grill 3, which allow you cook and bake pretty much anything. But the Sun Oven only works if there is sun, and the Volcano Grill can only bake one loaf of bread at a time. An Applebox Oven would work better because it can bake 3 loaves at a time. What it really boils down to is having cookers that fit your family size and needs AND having several different ways to cook your food, so if one way isn't working you have a back-up plan.

POWERLESS COOKERS

In most of the modern world, we have become accustomed to lighting a room with the flip of a switch and heating our food with the turn of a knob. Unfortunately, all this technology makes us more susceptible to cooking troubles during power outages. Most of these outages only last a few hours or days, but in severe cases they can last much longer. Are you prepared with ways to warm or cook your food without your modern kitchen appliances?

👍 SOLAR COOKING

If you live in a place where you have lots of sunny days, then you are going to LOVE solar cooking! The power in sunshine allows you to simmer, boil, and bake, and all without heating up your house and saving you money!

One of the added bonuses to solar cooking is the wonderful flavors that are achieved through sun-kissed cooking. It is so fun to put a frozen chicken or roast into your solar oven and several hours later have a beautifully browned, moist, juicy, and delicious meal. It is amazing! For those of you who have heard you can't bake bread in a solar oven, we want to put an end to that rumor right now. You not only can make beautiful bread, but you can cook corn-on-the cob and hard boil eggs without water. The possibilities are endless. You want to know a little secret? It is almost impossible to burn your food in a solar oven. Solar cooking is so easy and fun and something you are going to want to start using now because it is so satisfying!

ALL-AMERICAN SUN OVEN

This solar oven is the by far the best design on the market. It bakes much like a regular oven, with temperatures up to 400 degrees, and comes with a built-in thermometer. It has a self-leveling shelf to keep the food from spilling as the oven is tilted toward the sun with its adjustable leg, which can also be used to secure the oven during high winds. It's large enough to bake two loaves of bread, three racks of cookies, or up to a 21-pound turkey at a time. In addition, it is very easy to set up, take down, and transport. They are very user-friendly and well worth the money.

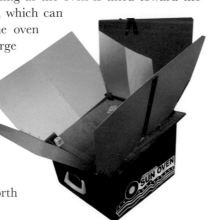

👍 STORE THIS!

APPLEBOX OVEN

The Applebox Oven is a fun and easy way to bake. It is made from a double thick, foil-lined apple box and is an inexpensive way to bake in an emergency. It bakes bread (up to 3 loaves at a time), rolls, muffins, casseroles, cookies, cakes, and anything you would bake in an oven, and uses only about half as much charcoal as Dutch oven cooking. To bake at 350° F, you would use 10–12 coals, which will give you about 35 minutes of cooking time. Baking once a day for 1 hour at 350° will use about 15 charcoals. In case you're wondering, that would be 16–20 pound bags of charcoal for a year, at a cost of about $60.

HINT: *Since they're made of cardboard and foil, they can be easily damaged by sharp objects. Store safely and keep foil and adhesive on hand for patching.*

THE VOLCANO GRILL

The Volcano Grill 3 is a compact, easily collapsible, portable grill that can use three different sources of fuel: propane, charcoal, and wood. It is easy to use and very versatile. In fact, it is the only cooker that we know of that lets you grill, boil, simmer, fry, smoke, use a wok or a Dutch oven, and bake.

It has some other unique features too:
- Its double-walled construction keeps the outside cool enough to touch with your hand.
- It can be used safely on most surfaces, including a plastic table.
- It conducts heat more efficiently than conventional grills, thus using less fuel.
- It has a vent system that allows you to control the heat.
- Clean out is easy; just dump out the ashes, wipe out, and store.

It is perfect for grilling at home, on a picnic or campout, or for emergency cooking. It is so fuel efficient that 15–20-lb. bags of charcoal would be enough to cook one hour a day for a year.

👍 AND THIS!

ROCKET STOVES

A rocket stove's unique design combines fuel and oxygen to create a very hot fire that uses very little fuel (twigs, sticks, pinecones, and charcoal). In fact, you can cook a big pot of food with just a handful of twigs! Rocket stoves can be large or small and made from metal #10 or 5-gallon cans—or even bricks. They can also be purchased commercially. They are a perfect accompaniment to a fireless cooker because you can bring the food to a boil very quickly, and then put it in the cooker to finish the cooking, thereby using very little fuel.

CAUTION: *Cooking on a rocket stove will turn your pots black.*

FIRELESS COOKERS

(also known as haybox cooker, icebox cooker, and wonder box)

Fireless cooking has been in use for hundreds of years. The cookers can easily be made of a box or ice chest with a couple of blankets and pillows, a pot wrapped in towels, or sewn from material and bean bag filling. Fireless cooking is essentially like crock pot cooking without the electricity; the secret being a quick heat up (on a stove for instance) and then letting the insulation do the rest of the cooking. To use, just boil your food for a few minutes in a pot with a tight-fitting lid, then quickly put the pot in your cooker; cover with pillow or other topper and leave for 2–4 times the usual cooking time. That's it; no stirring or burning! Food can be left up to 8 hours and still be hot and delicious. It is perfect for most foods, even bread, and is a great method to set yogurt. Best of all, it really saves on your cooking fuel!

DON'T FORGET THE WAPI

A Water Pasteurization Indicator, or WAPI, is a simple, inexpensive, reusable gadget that indicates when unsafe water has reached the pasteurization temperature of 149° and is safe to drink. It is made of a clear plastic tube containing a dab of green wax and weighted. It can be used when pasteurizing water in clear glass or plastic bottles and can be used directly in the sun or even inside solar ovens. The new Super WAPI can also be used in water heated with direct heat.

👎 NOT THIS!

There are two kinds of stoves that made our NOT THAT list: alcohol cookers and any stove for 72-hour kits.

Alcohol stoves, including canned heat (buffet food warmer fuel) and the DIY stove (made from a quart-sized paint can stuffed with a roll of toilet paper and smothered in rubbing or denatured alcohol), just don't live up to the hype. They only get hot enough to warm, not cook very small amounts of food. Another downfall is the DIY version burns through a quart's worth of alcohol in under two hours. There are much better options to choose from.

72-hour kit stoves: We are big believers in eat-on-the-move food, such as survival bars, so any type of cooker is not necessary and just takes up valuable space in your bag.

the rainy day fund you can eat

You are most likely familiar with the term "rainy day fund." It's a term used to describe a savings account that ensures you have money to use when times are tough. Think of your 90-day supply the same way: a way to ensure you have food to eat when times are tough. And it makes sense, right? You can't eat money, unfortunately. But you can have a supply of food to ensure you can feed your family following any job loss, family sickness, busy day, or personal emergency. Simply put, it's 90 days of meals that your family already eats. It includes foods that are shelf-stable, like the foods in your pantry, but it also includes foods that are in your refrigerator and freezer and foods that you pick fresh from your garden. It is 90 days of meals you can use every day and during life's emergencies, insuring that your family will stand strong through any storm.

life emergencies

Everybody has life emergencies that just affect your family. These unplanned events include things like a very busy day, illness, injury, surgery, death, or job loss. Knowing what a functional 90-day supply can do for you is essential knowledge for gathering the items that will help you, not hurt you.

emergency food VS. 90-day supply

In the previous chapter, we discussed that emergency food is for preparing for a natural disaster, but we all know there are more emergencies in life than those whipped up by Mother Nature.

What about the other life emergencies? You know, the ones that leave you rushing out to pick up some takeout? Wouldn't you like to have cheaper, faster options than the local burger joint? We thought so, and that is exactly what a good 90-day supply can offer you.

ABC News recently followed a family who loved to eat out to see which is really faster: eating out or cooking at home. They discovered that while people think it takes less time to go and pick up food, the truth is that cooking a simple meal at home is faster (and cheaper!).

never run out of anything.

A 90-day supply is also a great way to never run out of anything again. Don't you hate it when you're cooking a dish and discover that you don't have one of the ingredients? It can ruin your day, not to mention your meal! With a 90-day supply, you never run out of ingredients you regularly use, because you always have extras on hand. You will be able to make any favorite recipe at any time, with no more emergency trips to the store!

Did you know that grocery sales are cyclical?

Check out our guide on the next page to know when the best time to stock up on your favorites are!

1. start buying a few extras

A 90-day supply should consist of food your family already eats. Build a small supply of food that is part of your normal, daily diet. One way to do this is to purchase a few extra items each week to build a one-week supply of food. Then you can gradually increase your supply until it is sufficient for three months. These items should be rotated regularly to avoid spoilage.

Don't get hung up on shelf-stable meals. You've probably heard that your 90-day supply should be entirely shelf-stable, but since a 90-day supply is the food your family eats right now, doesn't that also include the food in your fridge and freezer as well as the pantry?

WAIT! You're giving me permission to have fresh and frozen meals as part of my 90-day supply?! YES! A 90-day supply is mostly for those life emergencies that interrupt your life today . . . while you still have electricity. If you don't have electricity for extended periods of time, then your long-term supply will step in and help. You can't spend so much of your time thinking of all the possible big Earth-encompassing emergencies that you don't think about the emergencies that can happen today at 5 o'clock when dinner needs to be on the table. So for that reason, yes, we give you concrete permission to count fresh and frozen food as part of your 90-day supply.

SHOPPING GROCERY SALES

Stock up on your favorite items when the price is right! Many grocery stores have cyclical sales that repeat every year. Use our helpful guide to decipher grocery store sales to save you money and hassle!

1-JANUARY

Welcome in the New Year with diet foods plentifully on sale ,and at the end of the month, Super Bowl favorites.

National Oatmeal Month: Most Quaker products will be on sale—more than just oatmeal!

Frozen Meals: Watch for single serving and family meals to be on sale.

Cereals: Special K, Kashi, Smart Start, Chex

Snacks: 100 Calorie Packs, Chips, Crackers, Snack Mixes

Dairy: Cheese, Yogurt, Sour Cream

Meat: Lunch Meat, Chicken Wings, Hot Dogs, Sausages, Petite Steaks, Pork Roasts, Beef Roasts, Ground Beef

Canned Goods: Chili, Canned Soups

Seasonal Produce: Oranges, Pears, Grapefruit, Tangerines, Broccoli, Carrots, Cauliflower, Celery, Chard, Collards, Kale, Kiwi, Avocado, Cabbage, Spinach

2-FEBRUARY

February is busier than you know! Not only is it Valentine's Day, it's the Chinese New Year and National Canned Food Month, along with National Hot Breakfast Month and American Heart Month. A good time to stock up.

Canned Goods: Canned Fruit, Pie Fillings, Vegetables, Tuna, Chicken, Salmon

Breakfast Items: Malt-O-Meal Cereals, Oatmeal, Eggo Waffles, Syrup, Pop Tarts

Valentine's: Chocolate, Hershey's, etc.

Chinese New Year: Soy Sauce, Teriyaki Sauce, Noodles, Canned Water Chestnuts, Stir-Fry Vegetables, Top Ramen

Seasonal Produce: Artichoke, Asparagus, Raspberries, Potatoes, Strawberries, Broccoli, Carrots, Cauliflower, Celery, Chard, Collards, Kale, Kiwi, Avocado, Spinach

3-MARCH

This month showcases Frozen Food Month, National Peanut Month, and, of course, St. Patrick's Day.

Frozen Food Month: Ice Cream, Frozen Vegetables (boxed, bag, or steam), Frozen Meals, Foster Farms Chicken, Waffles, Pizza

National Peanut Month: Peanut Butter, Peanuts

St. Patrick's Day: Potatoes, Corned Beef

Seasonal Produce: Artichoke, Asparagus, Avocado, Broccoli, Cabbage, Carrots, Cauliflower, Celery, Chard, Collards, Fennel, Kale, Leek, Lemons, Limes, Mushrooms, Spring Onions, Oranges, Peas, Radishes, Rhubarb, Spinach, Strawberries, Tangerines

4-APRIL

Easter, Passover, and Earth Day bring a great assortment of items on sale this month.

Easter/Passover: Ham, Eggs, Spices, Betty Crocker Boxed Potatoes, Maetza

Good Friday: Seafood, Frozen and Fresh Fish

Baking Supplies: Sugar, Spices, Baking Mixes, Chocolate Chips, Butter, Coconut, Marshmallows, Brownie Mix, Cake Mix

Earth Day: Organic Foods (both boxed and fresh)

Seasonal Produce: Artichoke, Asparagus, Avocado, Beets, Broccoli, Cabbages, Carrots, Grapefruit, Mushrooms, Onions, Peas, Rhubarb

5-MAY

Get ready to stock up on some great summer favorites! Memorial Day starts the great barbeque and grill season. Plus, it's Cinco de Mayo, and all of your Hispanic favorites will be on sale.

Memorial Day: BBQ Sauce, Condiments, Charcoal, Salad Dressing, Potato Chips, Dips, Grilling Meats, Hot Dogs, Ground Beef, Marinade, Salad Greens, Buns, S'mores (graham crackers)

Cinco De Mayo: Salsa, Tortillas, Chips, Canned Chiles, Canned Beans & Tomatoes, Enchilada Sauce, Cheese, Taco Seasonings, Taco Shells

Cereal: General Mills Products

Seasonal Produce: Artichoke, Asparagus, Avocado, Beets, Blackberries, Carrots, Green Beans, Lettuce, Sweet Vidalia Onions, Peas, New Potatoes, Raspberries, Strawberries, Tomatoes

6-JUNE

Summer sales are still going strong, along with National Dairy Month.

National Dairy Month: Eggs, Milk, Ice Cream, Cheese, Cream Cheese, Butter, Yogurt, Whipping Cream, Whipped Cream, Whipped Topping

Fourth of July Sales Start in the End of June: Hot Dogs, Hamburgers, BBQ Sauce, Ketchup, Condiments, Charcoal, Salad Dressing, Potato Chips, Dips

Seasonal Produce: Apricots, Blackberries, Blueberries, Cherries, Corn, Cucumber, Eggplant, Grapes, Honeydew, Nectarines, Peaches, Potatoes, Raspberries, Red Onions, Squash, Summer, Strawberries, Sweet Vidalia Onions, Tomatoes, Watermelon

7-JULY

Back to School sales at the end of the month, and it's time to stock up on ice cream since it's National Ice Cream Month.

National Ice Cream Month: Ice Cream, Ice Cream Novelties, Popsicles

More 4th of July BBQ Sales: Hot Dogs, Hamburgers, BBQ Sauce, Ketchup, Condiments, Charcoal, Salad Dressing, Potato Chips, Dips

Seasonal Produce: Asian Pears, Bartlett Pears, Blueberries, Corn, Cucumber, Eggplant, Figs, Garlic, Grapes, Green Beans, Nectarines, Onions, Red, Valencia Oranges, Peaches, Sweet/Bell Peppers, Plums, Potatoes, Summer Squash

8-AUGUST

Back to School sales are in full swing, including clearance on summer items.

Back to School Sales: Lunch Meat, Lunchables, Bread, Cold Cereal, Waffles, Granola Bars, Fruit Snacks, Pudding Cups, Peanut Butter, Jelly, Snacks

Seasonal Produce: Gravenstein Apple, Haas Avocado, Green Beans, Beans, Berries, Corn, Cucumber, Eggplant, Figs, Grapes, Melons, Onion, Peaches, Bartlett Pears, Bell Pepper, Plums, Raspberries, Squash, Summer, Tomatillo, Tomato

9-SEPTEMBER

Watch for a few last-minute Back to School sales.

Back to School Sales: Lunch Meat, Lunchables, Bread, Cold Cereal, Waffles, Granola Bars, Fruit Snacks, Pudding Cups, Peanut Butter, Jelly, Snacks

Seasonal Produce: Apples, Artichoke, Beans, Bell Peppers, Chili Peppers, Cucumber, Eggplant, Grapes, Onion, Valencia Orange, Asian Pears, Bartlett Pears, Pomegranate, Squash, Tomatillo, Tomatoes, Winter Squash

10-OCTOBER

This is the beginning of the best sales to hit all year. Also, watch for National Seafood Month and Adopt a Shelter Dog Month, when you can stock up on some of your dog's favorite treats and eats.

Halloween: Candy, Fresh Pumpkin

Beginning of the Baking Sales: Canned Pumpkin, Evaporated Milk, Sweetened Condensed Milk, Baking Chips

National Seafood Month: Frozen Shrimp, Fresh Salmon, Crab Legs

Adopt a Shelter Dog Month: Pedigree, Purina, Dog Treats

Seasonal Produce: Apples, Artichoke, Arugula, Beets, Broccoli, Brussels Sprouts, Cabbage, Chard, Chestnuts, Cranberries, Lemons, Parsnip, Pears, Pomegranate, Potatoes, Sweet Potatoes, Pumpkin, Spinach, Squash, Turnips, Yams

11-NOVEMBER

The best sales of the year are happening NOW! Basically, anything you need is probably on sale this month.

Hot Drinks: Cocoa, Coffee, Tea

Baking Sales in Full Swing: Nuts, Chocolate Chips, Evaporated Milk, Sweetened Condensed Milk, Coconut, Cake Mixes, Flavored Gelatin, Marshmallows

Canned Foods: Dinner Soups, Broth, Condensed Soups, Vegetables, Fruits, Spaghetti Sauce, Olives, Cranberry Sauce, Pumpkin

Frozen Items: Pies, Ice Cream, Whipped Topping, Frozen Vegetables

Meats: Turkey, Ham, Beef Roasts

Pantry Items: Stuffing Mixes, Gravy Mixes, Onion Soup Mix, Mashed Potatoes

Seasonal Produce: Pears, Beets, Broccoli, Brussels Sprouts, Cabbages, Carrots, Celery, Cranberries, Lemons, Oranges, Potatoes, Winter Squash, Yams

12-DECEMBER

Baking sales are still in full swing, along with great clearance items.

Holiday Dinner: Egg Nog, Deli Platters, Instant Potatoes, Gravy Mixes, Frozen Pies, Cranberry Sauce, Jello, Marshmallows, Sour Cream Dips, Crackers, Chips, Soda, Ham

Baking: Flour, Sugar, Butter, Cream, Cake Mix, Brownie Mix, Muffin Mix, Breads, Pie Crust, Marshmallows, Whipped Cream

Canned Foods: Soup, Broth, Condensed Milk, Vegetables, Fruits, Spaghetti Sauce

Seasonal Produce: Anjou Pears, Avocados, Bok Choy, Bosc Pears, Broccoli, Brussels Sprouts, Carrots, Cauliflower, Celery, Dates, Grapefruit, Kale, Kiwi, Kumquats, Lemons, Napa Cabbage, Oranges, Sweet Potatoes, Red Cabbage, Rutabaga, Savoy Cabbage, Spinach, Winter Squash, Yams, Turnips, White Potatoes

Oranges sliced for breakfast tomorrow

Waters perfectly chilled for lunches

Vegetables for Tuesday's dinner

Tonight's dinner, already started

With a great 90-day supply you always have a plan and everything you'll need to make the meals your family eats.

2. become the master of your food.

Welcome to stress-free cooking! Sounds like utopia, right? The secret to great meals is in the planning. The truth is, many people think they hate to cook when they just haven't figured out how to plan what to cook. When you plan your dinner menus ahead of time, you eat healthier, save money, reduce stress, and enjoy delicious meals. Menu planning is not brain surgery. When you see how simple it is to plan your own meals, you'll be amazed. Start with one week and work your way up to longer amounts of time.

menu planning 101

1. LOOK AT YOUR CALENDAR

Consulting the family calendar and weather before you plan your menu gives you the information to make better decisions. Give yourself a break on Monday (soccer night) with an easy meal, soup on Thursday during the storm, pizza on Friday with your family movie night, and a roast on Sunday when life has slowed down.

2. ASSIGN EVERY FOOD A JOB

With this rule, instead of seeing a jumbled mess of food in the fridge you will see Wednesday's broccoli, berries for yogurt parfaits, cheese for Tuesday's enchiladas, and a roast thawing for tomorrow's dinner. Planning for every aspect of the meal could save you $600 this year (the average cost Americans spend on spoiled food in one year).

3. VARIETY IS THE SPICE OF LIFE

Variety is what gives a menu all of its flavor. Be sure to vary the types of meals throughout the week. Mix it up, making sure you have different meats

(e.g. chicken, fish, beef, pork) and different types of meals (casseroles, roasts, salads, soups, etc.) in the course of the week.

4. START PREPARING EARLIER

This is your fighting chance to stick to your menu. If you're always thinking ahead, you are less likely to run out of time and energy. Plus, your kitchen stays much, much cleaner! Oatmeal can be started in a slow cooker the night before, sandwiches can be made at breakfast, and dinners can be prepped the night before or at lunchtime.

5. ROLL WITH THE PUNCHES

You don't have to be perfect! Not even close! There is no expectation that you never deviate from the menu. We totally understand that life happens. The value in menu planning doesn't come from managing the easily foreseeable (though if ignored, these will nail you). The value comes from managing the unforeseeable more effectively.

3. have a good backup plan

Stuff happens, but it doesn't need to get you down. With a great 90-day supply, you will have emergency meals you can fall back on when life gets in the way of your plans.

organized no-brainer meals

What is a no-brainer meal? No-brainer meals are those go-to meals you make when you don't have a lot of time to make dinner, the ones that are simple enough your 12-year-old could put them together. Everybody has them. We're just going to take those one step further and organize them so that most, if not all, of the ingredients are stored together, making the entire meal a no-brainer for someone to pick up and make.

We are big fans of no-brainer meals because

- Anyone can make them (even your children!)
- They are generally very fast and easy to put together for those extra-busy nights
- They're easy to rotate
- They are mostly shelf-stable for at least 3–6 months
- If you're sheltering at home for longer than two weeks, you'll need more easy meals

Believe it or not—you can actually purchase a lot of no-brainer meals at your local grocery store. Some of these may already be some of your family's favorites. Or you can make your own no-brainer meals. Think of recipes that you already use when you're in a hurry, meals like spaghetti, burritos, chili, soups, etc. These make great meals because they are quick and easy, you know you have all the ingredients to make them, and you know that your family will eat them.

freezer meals

Freezer meals are a perfect addition to any 90-day supply. They are little mess and no fuss, and most can be ready in under 30 minutes. Not even fast food or your local pizza joint can claim that, especially when you include driving and waiting time. We understand that freezer space can be similar to New York real estate, so make sure you are organized!

You can either
1. Purchase frozen meals from the grocery store,
2. Turn favorite family meals into freezer meals, or
3. Use a combination of buying and making

Purchasing Frozen Foods
These can include foods for breakfast, lunch, dinner, and dessert. They are fast and easy to prepare, have the instructions right on the box, and go on sale frequently, so it will be cheap and easy to stock up.

make your own freezer meals

Don't feel tied to your grocery store for good freezer meals. Good freezer meals are as close as the pancakes you made this morning or the chicken noodle soup you had for dinner. "Freezer cooking" is a great way to customize meals to fit your tastes, diet, and family size perfectly, resulting in homemade "convenience foods." You can even make slow cooker freezer meals.

If you want to get started with freezer meals, here are some tips:
1. Start with recipes your family already likes.
2. Test freeze your favorite recipe. To do this, next time you make it, simply put aside a small portion in a plastic container with a lid and freeze. Reheat and taste test.
3. Cook once and eat twice: the next time you make one of those recipes that freeze well, double it. Eat one now and freeze one in meal-sized portions for later. Nothing gets easier than that!

Don't want to shop or mess up your kitchen? In some areas there are meal prep kitchens that offer you a chance to cook in someone else's kitchen. They do all the shopping, the prep, and the clean-up. You just assemble the meals. But you pay more for the convenience—you can do it much cheaper at home.

Help to the rescue! Feeling overwhelmed by the whole idea of making fourteen dinners by yourself, turning your kitchen into a disaster zone, and loading up so many dishes in your sink, the sink falls out? (This really happened to Crystal!) Well, you are not alone. Get to together with friends or family to put together a variety of dishes to take home, or have a freezer meal swap. Making meals together takes half the time and is twice the fun!

your food storage
shopping guide

There are plenty of different food storage companies to choose from. The question is, which one is right for you and will give you the best deal? Don't worry if you have no idea how to answer that question. By the time you finish reading this chapter, you will.

learn the lingo

Food storage has a language all of its own. Just think, regular grocery stores don't call raisins "dehydrated grapes" like we would in the food storage world, and nobody refers to cans anymore by their numerical size. It's important to understand these terms to ensure you make the right choice and get the biggest bang for your buck.

POWDERS

The powdering process involves taking the product in a liquid state (milk as it is, eggs out of the shell and mixed together) and drying it, usually through a spray-drying process where the liquid is sprayed into a heated chamber and the water almost instantly evaporates, leaving behind tiny particles (the powder). Products that are powdered have a flour-like consistency and include butter, cheese, sour cream, eggs, margarine, and milk. But before we get your hopes up, it's important that you know that these powders (except for milk) were designed for and are best used in baked goods—not as butter on your toast or as sour cream on your potatoes.

INSTANT VS. NON-INSTANT

Any food that claims to be instant has gone through more processing than the non-instant variety to make it easier and faster to prepare. Because of the extra processing, these are usually more expensive and take more room to store. Non-instant foods are more compact and will usually provide greater bang for your buck and take less space on your shelf. Common foods that come in both instant and non-instant varieties are powdered milk, oats, rice, beans, etc.

FREEZE-DRIED VS. DEHYDRATED

Let's start out with what they have in common. Commercially dehydrated and freeze-dried foods are made from top-quality foods and are dried, through different processes, to have 98% of the water removed.

Freeze-dried foods are frozen first, and then the surrounding pressure is reduced to allow the frozen water in the food to go directly from ice to water vapor. Freeze-drying does not usually cause shrinkage or toughening of the food. It weighs much less than other preservation methods but needs just as much space to store as its fresh counterpart.

Dehydrated foods have their moisture removed by a combination of low to moderate heat and moving air. They are usually wrinkled in appearance, hard, and much smaller than their original size. In addition, because their bulk and weight have been greatly reduced, dehydrated foods are very compact for storing and require as little as $1/4$ the space of freeze-dried or fresh food. Dehydrated foods take longer to re-hydrate than freeze-dried but keep their shape better.

PRODUCT SIZE COMPARISONS

Pantry Can or #2.5 Can:
These cans are the size of a quart of paint, about 4 times smaller than the traditional #10 can, and are designed to fit better in your pantry. They are also called *My Choice*; *Everyday Can*, or *Small Can*.

Pouches or Mylar Bags:
These come in several sizes. The smallest contain only a few servings per pouch, like a sample size. These are not tear- or rodent-proof, so store them in another container to keep them safe.

#10 Can:
This is the traditional food storage, paint gallon–sized can. They are also called *Traditional* and *Large Can*. The cans hold over five pounds of grain, salt, etc. and under one pound of freeze-dried product.

BE SURE TO PICK UP SOME GAMMA LIDS FOR YOUR BUCKETS. THEY MAKE IT REALLY EASY TO OPEN AND CLOSE!

Bucket:
These can hold up to 6 gallons of product or about six times that in a #10 can. You can also find super pails where the food is packed in a mylar bag for an extra layer of protection.

label decoder

Many people underestimate the importance of reading the label before buying food. That's because they don't understand how vital the information on the label actually is. It will tell you how much food is really in the package, inform you of any extra ingredients they have added in (yes, you'd be surprised), and how much you're paying per serving. There's no getting around it—reading the label is a vital part of shopping—so, of course, we'll teach you everything you need to know about it.

KNOW WHAT IT IS REALLY COSTING YOU

With some food storage items, you'll want to know how they measure up to the price of fresh equivalents. Now, when we say fresh pricing we mean the fresh equivalent at the grocery store. For example, you'll want to know what the equivalent of a dozen powdered eggs costs compared to what a dozen fresh eggs will cost you at the grocery store. When you know that, you can make educated decisions on whether you should be using that product every day or waiting until there is an emergency or for when your stored food is cheaper to use than fresh. It won't save you any money to use products that cost MORE than what you can purchase at the grocery store. But it *will* save you money if you know which products will save you the most money to use every day.

READ THE LIST OF INGREDIENTS

Be sure to pay attention to the first three ingredients listed. Manufacturers list ingredients in order from most to least, meaning the first few ingredients usually make up the bulk of the food item. Therefore, if the first few ingredients are junk ingredients, then that's exactly what you're getting . . . PURE JUNK! You may find that refined sugar syrup is the first ingredient in your honey crystals, not honey— or that your favorite marinara powder's first ingredient is sugar, not tomatoes.

COMPARE WEIGHTS

Just because food is packaged in a certain size container doesn't mean it's full to the brim, and it certainly does not mean that different companies will have the same amount in each can (or bucket, pouch, box . . . you get the idea). So it's important to compare the weights of similar food storage products between companies and choose the one with the cheapest price per ounce.

COMPARE SERVING SIZES

Serving sizes vary between companies and products. We don't know about you, but when we think of a serving size we think in terms of quantity, what we will be really eating. For a meal, this is usually 1–2 cups of food. But this is not the case for most food storage companies. Some list the serving size by the prepared weight, some don't. Some use ounces, some use milliliters. Some do it by the piece, like 10 slices of banana. When we read the packaging of some "meals in a bucket" or "month of meals in a box," they say 325 meals. Really, in a 5-gallon bucket, how is that even possible? When reading the label you find out that a serving is ¼ cup milk or drink, or ⅓–½ cup of a pasta dish (doesn't say if this is dried or prepared). Read the label and you will find patterns in comparing one company to another.

food storage company secrets

You might be surprised to learn that even food storage companies have secrets. It's important to be realistic about these companies. Realize that while they are doing a great service providing us all with food storage, they are still companies trying to make a profit. Our job is to make sure that you can decipher the marketing from the truth.

#1. FOOD STORAGE COMPANIES DON'T WANT YOU TO KNOW THAT MOST OF THEM GET THEIR PRODUCT FROM THE SAME SOURCES.

If you knew this, you'd be more likely to shop between companies and find the best deals. Since we have worked with or for most of the major food storage companies, we know that some companies don't package any of their own food—instead they buy all of it from other food storage companies and mark up the price as resellers. No food storage company packages all of their food. Some package some of their food but still go to other companies for some products.

BOTTOM LINE: shop the best deal, not the best marketing story.

#2. FOOD STORAGE COMPANIES DON'T WANT YOU TO KNOW THAT YOU SHOULD PURCHASE THE BASICS FIRST.

We're always amazed at how many people buy things like brownie mix first before they buy the basics that will sustain life. Really, the basics—like wheat, beans, rice, pasta, and milk—are some of the least expensive items you'll buy . . . and have the lowest markup. Don't get us wrong, comfort foods are necessary and vital, but first you need to worry about sustaining life and then move onto comfort foods like brownies.

#3. FOOD STORAGE COMPANIES DON'T WANT YOU TO KNOW THAT SOMETIMES THEY TELL YOU TO USE MORE OF THE PRODUCT THAN YOU HAVE TO.

And why not? You'll go through the can a whole lot faster and need to buy more. Stick with us; we've actually tested all of these products and know the best ways to use them. For each product, we'll tell you the correct amounts to use to get the best results for your cooking and your pocketbook.

#4. FOOD STORAGE COMPANIES WITH INDEPENDENT DISTRIBUTORS AND PARTIES DON'T WANT YOU TO KNOW THAT THEY HAVE INCREDIBLY HIGH MARKUPS IN THEIR PRICING.

Those companies need high markups because when you purchase something from their independent distributors, the company has to pay the independent distributor a commission in both money and in free product, plus the consultant's upline (the people who signed them up) receive a commission, and of course the owners of the company need to make some money and pay their employees. It doesn't mean you should never buy anything from them—a good deal is a good deal. Just make sure that you purchase it because it's a good deal, not because your friend is selling it.

how to get a deal

It's getting close to the time for you to go shopping for your food storage. And when we say shopping, we mean it. When you go out to make a major purchase—say, a new car or a big appliance—you don't simply walk into the first showroom and purchase the first thing you see. A good shopper goes to a number of different stores, compares offers, and waits for good sales. The same applies when you're shopping for food storage. Before you start considering companies, you need to have a good sense of what kinds of deals are available.

DO SOME COMPARISON SHOPPING

All food storage companies are not created equally—especially in pricing. For a simple product like powdered eggs, the price can vary by at least *seven* dollars. Lucky for you, you can compare prices, sizes, and weights without ever leaving your house! Every food storage company has a website, so put on your slippers and do a little shopping from home.

COUPON CODES

Watch for coupon codes. Companies like Honeyville Grains have coupon codes every couple of months. Sign up on their website to receive the codes in your email. Thrive Life has Q-pons, which are monthly sales available to those signed up for their "Q" program (a monthly food storage program).

LOOK FOR GROUP BUY PROGRAMS

Companies like Emergency Essentials or Rainy Day Foods offer a simple, convenient, and affordable way for family, friends, and neighbors to work

together to obtain discounts on items relating to food storage and preparedness. Usually you'll work together with a "group leader" to meet the minimum purchase requirements, and when you do there are reduced prices and shipping is reduced or even free.

COMPARE SHIPPING RATES

Most food storage companies have variable shipping, meaning the more you spend, the more you pay in shipping. However, if you're making a large order, it may be worth it to use a company with flat rate shipping (like Honeyville Grains for only $4.49). Always be sure to compare the total price (items plus shipping) when trying to get the best deal.

WATCH FOR SALES

Did you know clothing and televisions aren't the only Black Friday items to watch for? Food storage companies also have Black Friday sales where preparedness and food storage prices are slashed. Emergency Essentials and Thrive Life are two such companies. New Year's is also a great time to watch for sales—food storage companies know a lot of people make it a resolution to get their food storage. Take advantage of case lot sales (if available) in your area. These usually take place in fall and spring.

what is
LONG-TERM
food storage?

Simply put, it's a collection of foods that are storable long term, are high in nutritional value, do not require refrigeration, and will sustain the basic needs of life. These basic foods include grains, pasta, beans, sugar or honey, milk, salt, and more. In addition, there are other shelf-stable foods, such as dehydrated fruits and vegetables, that when added to the basics open up the possibilities for real meals. Okay, we understand that "food that will sustain the basic needs of life" doesn't sound exciting. But we promise that we'll teach you how to turn these basics and other stable foods into meals you and your family are familiar with and will enjoy.

What are the basics for one person?

Start with the basics:

- *400 pounds of grains (wheat, oats, rice, corn, barley, pasta—get a good variety)*
- *60 pounds of beans*
- *60 pounds of sugar/honey*
- *12 pounds of non-instant powdered milk*
- *23 quarts of oil (oil, shortening, peanut butter)*
- *5 pounds of salt*
- *2 pounds of yeast*
- *1 pound baking soda*
- *1 pound baking powder*

Then add:

- *Vegetables: 8 #10 cans (3 potatoes; ½ can each of onion, celery, carrots, tomato powder)*
- *Fruits: 8 #10 cans*
- *Meats: 8 #10 cans of freeze-dried; 90 cans: 45 pints*
- *Dairy: cheese, eggs, etc. as needed*

5 IMPORTANT THINGS

a great long-term supply can do for you

We know that an emergency supply of food and water helps during a natural disaster and that a 90-day supply helps when recovering from a natural disaster that takes longer than two weeks or during a life emergency like job loss, sickness, or any other unplanned event. Here are five great reasons long-term food storage is so important.

Knowing what a functional long-term supply can do for you is essential knowledge for gathering the correct items.

---

1. A great long-term supply can help you every day, not just when the world ends, because it comprises basic ingredients you use every day.

When you understand what long-term food storage is—basic ingredients you use every day—it won't seem so scary. Think about it: ground wheat is simply flour, powdered milk can be used for fresh milk in any cooking, and the list goes on and on. Since these foods are also basic ingredients in many recipes, they can easily be rotated in your regular meals. Don't believe us? What if we told you that you are already eating these items? Do you ever use a pancake or muffin mix that says, "Just add water"? Surprise! That mix contains food storage ingredients like powdered eggs, powdered milk, and more. We'll give you a minute to get over the shock. So it turns out you already do use food storage—and like it!

2. A great long-term supply helps when a life emergency lasts longer than three months.

Sometimes finding a new job lasts longer than three months or medical bills are higher than you ever could have dreamed. Whatever the reason, if your life emergency, or the effects of it, are lasting longer than three months, you can delve into your long-term supply to help get you through it.

3. A great long-term supply can help you save money.

Cooking with and using items like powdered milk, powdered eggs, wheat, and many others can actually be cheaper than fresh ingredients—especially during times of inflation, droughts, and food shortages.

4. A great long-term supply helps during a nationwide crisis.

Whether the economy collapses, war breaks out that requires food rationing, or a large-scale drought diminishes food productions so drastically that it causes a famine in the land, you will still need food to provide for your family. A nationwide crisis like these would cause worldwide instability. It will take a long while to get back to "normal." No amount of money (or gold, for that matter) will provide food for your body if the shelves of your neighborhood store are empty and there are no trucks of food coming to refill them. Think about it, you can't eat money; you can't even burn enough of it to keep warm. Having food stored is the insurance you'll need to protect your family from "going without" during any long-term crisis.

5. A great long-term supply helps you eat healthier.

As we've discussed before, and as most people know, eating more whole grains and cooking from scratch is healthier. Whole grains and beans help you feel fuller faster, keep you full longer, keep you regular, and help decrease your chances of developing such diseases as adult-onset diabetes, some cancers, and heart disease. Also, eating whole grains and beans now will prepare you (and your digestive tract) for the possibility of living off these items later.

how to create a great
LONG-TERM
food storage?

RULE NO. 1: START WITH THE BASICS

Why the basics? Because they are the easiest to store (most can even be stored in a garage); they have the longest storage life (20+ years); they provide all the nutrients and calories you need to survive (sprouting gives vitamin C); and they are by far the cheapest way to store food. You may not be excited about what you can make with the basics, but you will be grateful that you have something to put on your plate, and with a few other inexpensive ingredients (which of course we will share with you), you will be able to make some simple and even tasty meals. Because these basics are the foundation for pretty much everything we eat, they are not hard to rotate. Just be sure you keep some extra on hand of the things you are rotating so you don't go below your minimum, and replace them in a timely manner.

HINT: Buy what you like. In other words, if you don't like black beans, don't buy black beans. Be sure to buy a variety of grains, pasta, and beans you like.

RULE NO. 2: AVOID THE #10 CAN TRAP

Remember that every food storage company would love for you to purchase everything freeze-dried or dehydrated, but it's not necessary. In fact, if everything you store long-term is freeze-dried or dehydrated, you will need to store a boatload of water (we're only half kidding . . . about the boat, not the extremely large amount of water you'd have to store). How about if you store some canned goods too! They are easily rotated, and you can use the liquid in the cans as part of your water. After tasting and testing freeze-dried, dehydrated, and canned, we realized that there are really good- and really bad-tasting products in each category. Lucky for you, we are going to share this information so that you can get the biggest bang for your buck: money-wise and space-wise. You'll learn which products we like and why, how using some of your long-term supply right now can start saving you money, and lots of useful tips along the way.

RULE NO. 3: START COOKING AT HOME

Using a long-term supply successfully means you'll need to start cooking at home more. Remember, a basic long-term supply is full of basic ingredients that you can use in any recipe—basic ingredients you can pronounce, unlike prepackaged food from the store. Cooking at home gives you more control over the ingredients you are feeding to your family. Aside from the health benefits, homemade recipes are always much more cost effective. You just pay for the ingredients, not the packaging, the cost of production, or the advertising, or all the other costs that a company charges to its consumers. If you are trying to save some money in this economy, then this can be a great addition to your list of frugal practices. Did you know a family of four can save over $200 a year by making homemade bread? Think of all the food storage you can buy with that extra money!

MAKING MEALS

If you aren't excited about eating meals with just plain food storage, we don't blame you, but having those basics gives you a great foundation for making delicious meals, and that is where the next step comes in: thinking in terms of meals. Instead of thinking of wheat, think sandwich bread, artisan bread, pancakes, muffins, waffles, white sauce, tortillas, crackers, cookies, etc. Instead of beans, think soups, burritos, salads, gravy, and even brownies (that's right, we said brownies). In our recipe section, we will show you that by adding, fruits, vegetables, seasonings, sauces, and spices, you can really make delicious meals with your basics.

PROTECTING
your long-term food storage

ROTATING YOUR FOOD STORAGE

There are **three basic camps of thought** when it comes to rotating your food storage:

1. As you use it, you replace it one can or bottle, or better yet, one meal at a time.

2. Every 5–10 years you just replace it all at once.

3. You never replace it, and when it comes time to use it, you either eat the off-color, mushy food, give it to someone who has nothing to eat, or throw it away, which would be a terrible waste.

We hope you are so excited about our program you choose Option 1. If, however, you aren't sure, let's see if we can use a little of our magical food storage powers to persuade you to at least giving it a try.

Using and replacing your food storage has so many benefits. Besides being cheaper and healthier, you are acting on your belief that food storage is important, important enough to save and sacrifice for. This action includes learning to cook with it, and by doing that you will quickly become at ease with baking a loaf of bread or maybe even making tortillas. Your family and friends will be amazed at your cooking skills as you produce delicious meals made from "food storage," making them believers too. As a side benefit, you learn to replace any good, bad, and yucky recipes or ingredients with ones you love. As you do this, you will want to buy more food so you can make more delicious meals. And it goes on and on and you will be happy and blessed. Okay, so maybe that was a little much, but we had to give it a shot. Really try it; you just may like it. If after this you still think you won't rotate, then go for the products that have the longest shelf life.

STORAGE LIFE

You need to take into consideration that canned, dehydrated, and freeze-dried products have a much shorter shelf life than the basics. For instance, on average, these products, if stored properly in a cool, dark place, will store for the following times:

- Canned meats, fruits, and vegetables: 2–5 years
- Commercially freeze-dried products: 10–15 years
- Commercially dehydrated fruits and vegetables: 10 years
- Home-canned products: 2–5 years
- Home-dehydrated fruits and vegetables: 2 years.

If they have been properly processed and stored (with no air, light, or humidity, and kept cool), they will still be safe to eat long after this time, but they may look, smell, and taste different. So, if you are not using this food, it will grow yucky over time and need to be replaced.

MAKE A COMMITMENT

You now know more about how to plan and begin a great long-term food supply than 90 percent of the people who will ever have or try to have a long-term food storage. In short, you are ready to get going. So right now, this very minute, make a commitment to yourself to make this happen. Our hunch is that in no time you'll have a fantastic long-term food supply by your side, saving you money, helping you eat healthier, and preparing you for any emergency that may come your way.

A GRAIN
of truth

AGAINST THE GRAIN? We're not, and we'll tell you why. All large populations of healthy people, throughout verifiable human history, have obtained the bulk of their calories from grains. There can be problems for some when eating some kinds of grain, but for the rest of us the benefits of all grains far outweigh the negatives. Grains are cheap and easy to store. For the vast majority of us, whole grains can and should be the foundation of our everyday lives and long-term food storage.

GRAINS ARE AN ESSENTIAL PART OF YOUR FOOD STORAGE.

Grains are a perfect solution to food storage because they provide a relatively high source of calories for a very low cost. And they can be stored (for not just days but decades) for use in times of need. How much should you store for a year? Four hundred pounds, or roughly eight buckets of grain, the bigger the variety the better. If you are planning to make bread, roughly half of that should be wheat. What else can you use and store besides wheat? Barley, pasta, corn, oats, rice, quinoa, spelt, and kamut, to name a few.

THE BENEFITS OF GRAINS.

In societies where people consume a diet founded on grains, they suffer from relatively few of the chronic illnesses that plague our society today. This was also true of peoples of all the great civilizations of the past. Eating whole grains can help you lower your cholesterol, improve blood pressure, prevent birth defects, keep your digestive tract—shall we say—regular, keep you fuller longer, help you lose weight, fight diabetes, strokes, and heart disease—and the list goes on and on. Whole grains don't contain one magical nutrient that fights disease and improves health. It's the entire package, all the elements intact and working together, that's important. With benefits like those, who wouldn't want grains in their food storage?

ARE GRAINS REALLY BAD FOR US?

There are many people these days trying to convince us that all grains are bad for us. This just isn't true. While we do not doubt that some individuals are sensitive to specific grains, and some are gluten intolerant or function best without wheat, the wholesale condemnation of grains goes against both human physiology and human history. The fact that some people do better without gluten is not nearly as important as the fact that up to 80% of all chronic illness can be resolved with a whole-grain, plant-based diet.

Here are a few of their arguments and our take on them.

Grains and other starchy plant foods provide significantly more calories than the typical vegetable or even fruit, allowing humans to satisfy their energy requirements in a much more efficient way. These foods can also be more easily stored for use in times of cold or famine. Human civilization is not possible without the cultivation of grains. They are, indeed, the "staff of life."
— *Food expert Harold McGee*

the grain rules.

Grains have changed: While it is true that all plant and animal foods have changed over time and that some of the changes may not be entirely positive (can we say GMO?), these changes, natural or not, do not mean the grain itself is bad or toxic for us. Most people can handle the imperfections in foods, yet others have problems with foods that are known to be health promoting. This can be due to genetics, use of medications, or environmental factors, and sometimes it is caused by a poor diet—the type of diet most Americans eat.

Grains make people fat: Refined grains, which are the bulk of what most people consume, have been linked to obesity, heart disease, diabetes, and lots more. Whole grains, on the other hand, have the opposite effect.

Eating grains makes people sick: It may be that the poor quality of our diet causes some people to have problems digesting the gluten and phytic acid found in some grains. The answer is not to attack the grain, but to change the diet or the way the grains are prepared. If grains are prepared by soaking or sprouting first, and if bread is risen slowly, gluten and phytic acid are sharply reduced, and vitamin and mineral content is increased. When introducing whole grains to your diet, do it a little bit at a time, letting your body get used to the additional fiber, and drink lots of water. That way you won't have to worry about any gas or bloating.

INGRAINED

In the end, here's our pitch for eating whole grains.

- Grains can provide key nutrients (helping prevent malnutrition) and should be the foundation of your food storage.
- Grains are low in caloric density (helping prevent excess body fat).
- Grains can help decrease the risk for chronic disease (cancer, heart disease, diabetes).

Of course, if you can't tolerate grains, or any other food, and they make you feel bad, stop eating them!

However, if you can tolerate them, don't fall for the hype. Whole grains aren't the next dietary evil. Instead, look for ways to include them in your diet and watch your health improve.

1. Store grains you currently eat.

Don't kid yourself: if you don't currently eat barley, don't store it just because you think you should. Buying grains that you really won't use is a waste of money, time, and food. The best grains you can store are the grains you and your family are already familiar eating. As you'll see, the grains you can store in your food storage are a lot more common than you think.

2. Use ancient grains to accent basic grains—not replace them.

While ancient grains are packed with nutrition, ancient grains haven't been in vogue long enough to do proper testing on storage life. In fact, most food storage companies haven't been in business long enough to test claims of storing for up to 30 years. And grains like quinoa can be very expensive to store.

3. Plan for variety

Nobody wants to eat the same thing over and over again. Every grain has positive uses. Oats can be used in cookies and baking and as a breakfast cereal. Wheat can be ground into flour that can make amazing breads or baked items, or can be used whole as a side dish or cereal. And who can forget some cornmeal for cornbread, or pasta for a quick dinner. Make sure you have all the different grains you'll need to fill all of your different cooking, baking, and side dish needs.

BASIC *grains*

We love barley in soups (who doesn't love a good Beef & Barley soup?), cereal, and gluten-free baking.

Don't let the name fool you! You probably know it better as Cream of Wheat or Farina, and it makes a delicious warm cereal.

Oat groats are the whole oat grain. Groats take longer to cook than rolled oats, but they do make a tasty warm cereal.

	BARLEY	CORNMEAL	GERMADE	OATS	OAT GROATS
FIBER	👍 32 grams	6 grams	3.3 grams	8 grams	16 grams
PROTEIN	👍 23 grams	11 grams	19 grams	12 grams	👍 26 grams
STORAGE LIFE	8 years	25 years	8 years	👍 30 years	👍 30 years
PRICE PER CUP	$0.85	$0.91	$0.90	👍 $0.58	👎 $0.84
GLUTEN-FREE	no	yes	no	yes	yes

Cornmeal is a course flour made from dried corn. It's used in baked goods (like corn bread and pancakes), as a coating for meats, and to keep your artisan breads from sticking to the pan.

Oats are used in the common breakfast cereal. You can use them in baking (cookies and breads) and of course for breakfast.

RICE VS. INSTANT RICE

You will always get the best deal buying the regular product vs. the instant product, so if you like getting the best deal (like us), store this!

Anytime you buy instant anything, you will be paying a lot more for the product (in this case, 50 percent more) and getting a lot less in the can!

STORE THIS

NOT THAT

ba•sic grains: Basic grains are food storage classics—the kind your mother and grandmother stored. They are a food storage tradition because they are inexpensive and nutritious and most store for a long time. As an added benefit, they are so easy to use that they can and should be used every day. They are tried, true, and tested candidates for your food storage.

You can pop this corn for a tasty snack or grind it and use it to make bread.

White rice is cheap and cooks quickly. You can also use it as a side dish, in gluten-free cooking, and in various desserts.

White flour is the most common—however, it doesn't store very long, and you can always grind wheat to make flour!

PASTA	POPCORN	BROWN RICE	WHITE RICE	WHEAT	WHITE FLOUR
3.4 grams	13 grams	3.5 grams	0.6 grams 👎	23 grams 👍	3.4 grams
14 grams	11 grams	5 grams	4.2 grams	30 grams 👍	13 grams
30 years 👍	10 years	5 years 👎	30 years 👍	30 years 👍	5 years 👎
$0.98	$1.08	$0.80	$0.79	$0.75 👍	$0.60
no	yes	yes	yes	no	no

While you can make your own pasta, we think you'll really enjoy having some dried pasta on hand for convenience.

Brown rice is whole grain rice. It has a mild, nutty flavor and is chewier and more nutritious than white rice, but goes rancid much faster.

👍 STORE THIS!

Wheat is a perfect choice for your food storage! It's packed with great nutrition, is inexpensive, stores for a long time, and can be used in a wide variety of dishes.

WHITE WHEAT VS. RED WHEAT

The two wheats contain similar amounts of protein and fiber, but they differ in color and taste. White wheat is golden in color and has a subtle flavor that is easily disguised in baked goods, Plus, it makes light fluffy bread. So if you're worried about taste (like us), store this!

Hard red wheat is reddish in color and has a stronger, nuttier flavor that is hard to disguise in baked goods without mixing in at least half white flour, which also cuts the nutrition by half. Bread made from this wheat can be dense and dry.

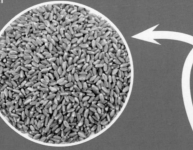

STORE THIS   **NOT THAT**

ANCIENT *grains*

an·cient grains: Ancient grains are more than just relics from the past that have stood the test of time; they are cereals and seeds that have a robust texture and stellar nutritional profile. However, these grains have not had adequate testing on REAL storage life. So we went very conservative on the storage life so you don't get caught with a rancid grain supply.

Amaranth, like quinoa, is a seed and not actually a grain. The Aztecs used it long ago in cooking and religious ceremonies. It's great as a cereal or in gluten-free baking.

Although millet is most often associated as the main ingredient in bird seed, it is not just "for the birds." Creamy like mashed potatoes or fluffy like rice, millet is a delicious grain.

Some of the earliest recordings of spelt appear in the Bible. Spelt is actually a cousin of wheat and can be used similarly.

	AMARANTH	KAMUT	MILLET	QUINOA	SPELT
FIBER	13 grams	17 grams	17 grams	12 grams	👍 19 grams
PROTEIN	👍 26 grams	👍 27 grams	👍 22 grams	👍 24 grams	👍 25 grams
STORAGE LIFE	👎 5 years	👎 5 years	👎 5 years	👎 5 years	👎 5 years
PRICE PER CUP	$1.61	$0.67	$1.20	👎 $3.70	👎 $2.78
GLUTEN-FREE	yes	no	yes	yes	no

Kamut is a brand of khorasan wheat. It is a close relative to wheat and is about the same shape as a wheat seed, but a Kamut kernel is more than twice as big.

Most folks call quinoa a grain, but it's actually a seed — one that originated thousands of years ago. It's treasured because of its nutritive value (more protein than any other grain or seed!).

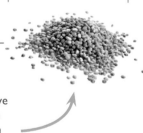

QUINOA—TO STORE OR NOT TO STORE?

Quinoa is very popular right now but it is also very, very expensive—at least $1.00 more per cup serving than any other grain! That means for a family of four, you're paying $6 more per meal every time you eat it! (And you could get a whole can of a basic grain of your choice for $6!) If you want to store it, make sure it's because you like it, not just because you're buying into the hype. And remember, ancient grains are a great accent to the basics!

GRAIN MILLS

To make the best use of your grains, be sure to invest in a grain mill to grind your grains into flour.

12-cup grain hopper

Adjustable grinding speeds from coarse to fine

20-cup flour canister

BEST GRAIN MILL: NUTRIMILL

Amazon, $219.99 with free shipping

The Nutrimill grain mill is by far our favorite! It has the largest grain hopper (holds up to 12 cups) and flour canister (holds up to 20 cups). Plus, it runs $20 cheaper than the competition and takes up half the space on your counter. It's as quiet as grain mills go (only 50 decibels) and does the best job grinding grains—grinding some as fine as cornstarch! Add in a lifetime warranty and you have your next grain mill!

Adjustable grinding speeds from coarse to fine

2-cup grain hopper

20-cup flour canister

BEST STARTER MILL: BLENDTEC KITCHEN MILL

Amazon, $179.95 with free shipping

The Blendtec Kitchen Mill is a great starter mill! It is inexpensive and compact, does a five-star job grinding, and can hold up to 20 cups in the flour canister. It is louder than the Nutrimill (about 68 decibels) and the grain hopper only holds 2 cups, which means you'll need to keep refilling it while you are grinding until the canister is full.

Flour comes out here—have a bowl to catch it!

1-quart grain hopper

Hand crank

Super grip dual clamp. Will not slip like other hand mills.

BEST HAND GRAIN MILL: WONDERMILL JR./DELUXE

Wondermill JR Amazon, $129.95/Wondermill JR Deluxe Amazon, $219.95

Finally, a sturdy, well-built, functional, portable, hand-cranked grain mill that does more than a superb job and does not cost a fortune! It grinds fine flour or coarse cracked grains for cereals. It will grind wheat, rice, popcorn, and other grains. The deluxe model will also grind legumes and beans as large as garbanzos, as well as grind oily seeds, nuts, and herbs. Simply load the easy-fill hopper, turn the handle, and you'll get flour. There are no small parts or gaskets to misplace. And cleaning the WonderMill Junior is quick and easy.

MILL THIS . . .

Non-oily grains and legumes like wheat, rye, spelt, millet, rice, corn, beans, quinoa, amaranth, and oats.

NOT THAT . . .

Oily grains like chia, flax, nuts, coffee beans, Hemp seed, and Goji berries. Grains with high moisture content, spices, seeds, and sugar.

Beans

THE ULTIMATE SUPERFOOD

A PERFECT PAIRING

Are beans a complete protein? No, but when eaten with nuts, seeds, or whole grains, within two days of beans they become one.

DID YOU KNOW?

BEANS ARE FOR MORE THAN JUST DINNER

This is food storage's best-kept secret! You can actually use beans to replace the fats (butter, oil, or shortening) in your baked goods! We promise that once you learn the secret of bean butter (page 52), you'll become addicted to this easy way to cut the fat and add a nutritional punch to your favorite foods!

MORE COST-EFFECTIVE THAN MEAT

Beans are very low in sodium and offer many of the same nutrients as meat, but without the fat and cholesterol. In fact, each half-cup serving of dry beans provides six to seven grams of protein and meets at least 10% of the Recommended Dietary Allowance (RDA) for protein, yet costs about 20 cents per serving.

SUPERFOOD

Beans are a superfood and one of the most nutritionally complete foods available. In fact, no other food comes close to beans in providing protein, fiber and antioxidants in such high quantities. Beans give you a lot of bang for your buck. They are low in cost, cholesterol free, low in fat (2–3%), and high in fiber, protein, carbohydrate, folate, and many trace minerals. In fact, because beans are high in fiber and low in fat, they can actually help lower your cholesterol.

EATING THREE CUPS OF BEANS PER WEEK WILL

Balance blood sugar by digesting slowly (good for diabetics) • Reduce risk of cancers and heart disease • Lower blood pressure • Lower cholesterol and triglycerides (heart healthy) • Prevent and cure colon & bowel problems

BEANS, BEANS, THE MAGICAL FRUIT, THE MORE YOU EAT THE MORE YOU . . .

Beans contain sugars that our digestive tracts lack the enzymes to digest. To fight the noisy side effects of beans, you need to eat more beans! We know it sounds counterintuitive, but it's true! If you gradually increase the amount of beans you eat over several weeks, you will overcome this. To help in the interim, you may want to invest in some Beano (an over-the-counter supplement that contains a natural food enzyme that helps prevent gas before it starts).

3 EASY WAYS *to* STORE BEANS

DRIED BEANS are beans that are uncooked, hard, and small. They can take longer to cook but are much cheaper in price and store for 30 years.

COOKED BEANS can be purchased in the store in 15.5-ounce cans and are completely cooked. You can open, reheat, and eat. These have a best by date of a few years.

INSTANT BEANS have been cooked and then freeze-dried. They need to be rehydrated before eating.

DRIED BEANS

COOKED BEANS

INSTANT BEANS

BEAN EQUIVALENTS

1 #10 CAN OF DRIED BEANS

23 15.5-OUNCE CANS OF COOKED BEANS

3.5 #10 CANS OF INSTANT BEANS

If you store dried beans instead of instant beans in your food storage, you could

SAVE ALMOST $500 PER PERSON!

That is enough for a nice family vacation or a lot more food storage!

YEAR SUPPLY PRICE DIFFERENCES

12 #10 CANS OF DRIED BEANS
$180

$264

276 15.5-OUNCE CANS OF COOKED BEANS

42 #10 CANS OF INSTANT BEANS
$630

Mix and match dried and cooked beans for all the benefits!

store this NOT THAT

 DRIED BEANS: You just can't beat the price, storage life, or the small amount of storage space they will take on your shelves. They can take a long time to cook, but they can also be done in as little as 45 minutes.

 COOKED BEANS: If you're turned off by the cooking time of dried beans and want beans that can be eaten right away, then these are your best option. You don't need any extra time or money. Plus, if you shop sales you can get a great price on these.

 INSTANT BEANS: Can you say rip-off? They cost almost 5 times the price of dried beans, but they still take 20 minutes before you can eat and a lot of water to rehydrate!

Bean there, done that?

LEARN HOW TO USE BEANS IN PLACE OF BUTTER AND OIL

1. If your recipe calls for oil or melted butter, you are going to use a bean purée. You can make a bean purée by simply pouring a can of beans into your blender (liquid and all) and puréeing. Then, to make your recipe, use the same amount of bean purée as your recipe calls for oil. So if your recipe calls for ¼ cup oil, you will use ¼ cup bean purée.

2. If your recipe calls for shortening, butter, or softened butter, you are going to use cooked, drained beans. We can't use a bean purée to replace butter or shortening because the consistency is not the same and will ruin your baked good. To make your recipe, use the same amount of beans as your recipe calls for butter. So if you're making cookies, and the original recipe calls for creaming one cup of butter with the sugar, you are going to use one cup of your cooked, drained beans and cream it in with your sugar. Don't worry, there won't be any bean chunks by the time you are done mixing your dough.

3. When wondering which beans to use—you are going to match color for color. If it is a chocolate cake, use black beans. If it is a spice cake, use pinto beans. If it is a white cake, use white beans. You can always use white beans in something darker like chocolate cake, but you can't use black beans in your white cake. Your family will wonder what all of those black specks are. To be safe, you can use white beans in almost anything.

4. Beans will give your baked goods a very moist cake-like texture. So if you are making a baked good that is meant to be chewy (like brownies or chocolate chip cookies), you can always use half oil/butter and half beans. It will still be chewy and you'll still be saving money and adding fiber and protein! Remember, we're not big into all or nothing—even a little or half is better than nothing, and it's important that your family likes what you make!

5. When you try using beans for butter and oil and discover that you love it, as we are confident you will, you may want to cook large batches of beans and freeze whole beans and bean purée in smaller portions for easy use in your baking.

Cooking with your beans

LEARN TO LOVE COOKING DRIED BEANS

soaking beans

Soaking is an important step in the bean cooking process. Soaking has two major benefits: It reduces the cooking time and it breaks down the compounds in beans that cause gas. The longer beans soak, the more the gas-producing compounds break down. Beans will double or triple in size, depending on which soaking method you use, so it's important to use a large enough pot when soaking beans. There are three soaking methods you can use, the Hot Soak Method, the Traditional Soak Method, and the Quick Soak Method.

The Hot Soak Method is the recommended method because it reduces cooking time and gas-producing compounds the most and produces consistently tender beans.

The Hot Soak Method
1. Place beans in a large pot and add 10 cups of water for every 2 cups of beans.
2. Heat to boiling and boil for an additional 2 to 3 minutes.
3. Remove beans from heat, cover, and let stand for 4 to 24 hours.
4. Drain beans and discard soak water.
5. Rinse beans with fresh, cool water.

The Traditional Soak Method
1. Pour cold water over beans to cover.
2. Soak beans for 8 hours or overnight.
3. Drain beans and discard soak water. (NOTE: cold water starts but does not complete the rehydration process, so the beans will appear wrinkled after soaking. They will fully rehydrate during cooking.)
4. Rinse beans with fresh, cool water.

The Quick Soak Method
1. Place beans in a large pot and add 6 cups of water for every 2 cups of beans.
2. Bring to boil and boil for an additional 2 to 3 minutes.
3. Remove beans from heat, cover, and let stand for 1 hour.
4. Drain beans and discard soak water.
5. Rinse beans with fresh, cool water.

cooking beans

STOVETOP:
After soaking the beans, rinse and cover with new water, covering the beans with one inch of water. Bring the beans to a boil and then gently simmer for the rest of cooking. Cook the beans for one hour, and then begin checking for doneness. Depending on their age, size, and variety, beans can take anywhere from an hour to three hours to cook through. Be patient. Keep the beans at a gentle simmer and taste frequently as they start to become tender. Add more water as needed to keep the beans submerged and stir occasionally.

SLOW COOKER:
3½-quart or smaller slow cooker for 1 pound of beans or less,
OR
5-quart or larger slow cooker for 2 pounds of beans or more

After soaking the beans (optional), transfer the beans to the slow cooker. If you haven't already done so, rinse and pick over the beans, then transfer them to a slow cooker. Cover with water. Pour enough water over the beans to cover them by about 2 inches. Add any spices or onions. Cook on low for 6 to 8 hours.

PRESSURE COOKER:
Soaking your beans is completely optional when using a pressure cooker, which can save a lot of time! Check your manual for cooking times and pressure release methods. But if your beans have been soaked they can cook in as little as 5 minutes, or 45 minutes unsoaked. Also, be sure to add 1 tablespoon of oil to your beans to keep the foam down.

Cooking tip: Never add salt until the end of the cooking process—it makes the beans tough.

MILK
IT DOES A FOOD STORAGE GOOD.

All it takes are a few simple ingredients and a little know-how to turn powdered milk into sweetened condensed milk, evaporated milk, condensed soups, and something drinkable.

DREAMING OF A GLASS OF POWDERED MILK?

Probably not, and we completely understand. For years, powdered milk was just plain yucky and the stuff nightmares are made of. If you are one of the many that cringe when you hear the words "powdered milk," we are happy to tell you times have changed. Today's powdered milk has evolved and actually tastes like, well, milk!

Contrary to popular belief, powdered milk is very easy to use. It requires no special tools and can be made by the glass or by the gallon for drinking. In fact, it is great for mixes and can be used in any recipe calling for milk. Because of its convenience, ease of use, and nutritional benefits, there is no doubt that powdered milk will play an important role in your food storage.

In fact, because milk is a complete protein (meaning it has all eight essential amino acids) and has carbohydrates, vitamins, and minerals, you could survive for a while by just drinking milk, but who would want to? Milk can be used to drink, but why not use it to add balance and variety to your meals? Powdered milk can be used to make so many foods, such as breads, soups, sauces, yogurt, cheese, and desserts, including delicious homemade ice cream!

If you think you already know all about powdered milk, and were considering skipping the next few pages, think again. We've discovered some interesting and deceptive details in our research that just may change your mind about the kind of milk you want to store and how much you need to store. So let's get started separating fact from fiction in the whitewashed world of powdered milk, and then introduce you to all of your many, many dairy options.

POWDERED MILK

All Powdered Milks Are NOT Created Equal

That's right, folks, there are big differences in powdered milks. Some are pretty comparable to a real glass of milk and others are not. Some mix with cold water and some with warm. Some you can cook with or make yogurt, some you can't. Some are a good value, even cheaper than fresh and worth using daily, while others are REALLY not. Some store for 5 years and some for 20+. All can be used for drinking—which brings up the taste factor. None of these have the "gag-me" flavor anymore; in fact, most taste pretty good. The problem is that the "milk" that most people think tastes best is really more of a milk-looking sugary drink. (Say what?!)

That being said, we are all about the power of choice. We just want you to be fully aware of what you're really getting with each product so you can store enough of the milk that your family really wants.

Instant vs. Non-Instant Milk . . . What's the Difference?

Instant and non-instant powdered milk are both made from non-fat milk. They are just processed a little differently. They are both available in vitamin-fortified (vitamins A and D) and non-fortified versions and they can both be used for drinking, cooking, and making yogurt and cheese. Once mixed, there is no measurable difference in taste, texture, usability, or nutritional value. They both store 20+ years in cool conditions. There are, however, major differences in mixing, cost, and space needed to store it.

INSTANT POWDERED MILK

Much like popped popcorn, instant milk is puffed up, making it light and fluffy. It weighs less but takes up more space than non-instant powdered milk, so you get less in a #10 can. (Think the powdered milk you can buy in your local grocery store.) It takes 4–7 tablespoons to make one cup of milk for drinking and double that amount for cooking. It dissolves quickly and easily in cold water with hardly the stir of a spoon. It is ready to drink or use immediately.

- light and fluffy
- dissolves quickly in cold water
- 4–7 tablespoons per cup for drinking
- double amount when used in cooking
- averages 2 gallons of milk per #10 can
- more expensive: $7–$10 per gallon
- 10 #10 cans per person, per year (1 cup per day)

NON-INSTANT POWDERED MILK

Non-instant powdered milk is like unpopped popcorn kernels. It is denser and heavier than its "popped" counterpart. It looks and feels like fine, squeaky powder. It only takes 3 tablespoons of powder to make a cup of milk, so more servings fit in a #10 can. For best results, it needs to be mixed with warm water using a wire whisk and chilled overnight.

- fine, dense, and heavy
- dissolves in warm water
- 3 tablespoon per cup
- averages 3.5 gallons per #10 can
- most cost effective ($2–$8 per gallon)
- about 50% cheaper to use than instant
- 6 #10 cans per person, per year (1 cup per day)

Check out our best tips for making drinkable milk from your powdered milk on page 109.

MILK ALTERNATIVES

Milk alternatives go by many names and are sometimes even marketed as real milk, so it's important to understand what it really is and how to spot it. It weighs and mixes the same as non-instant milk and is cheaper, but it has fewer calories. Alternatives have only half the carbohydrates and protein and only one third of the calcium that powdered milk has, and they only store 5 years in optimal cool storage.

We like to compare milk alternatives and milk as you would Tang and real orange juice. While Tang is orange and a drink, it contains only a small portion of real juice. Conversely, orange juice is just that—juice from an orange, containing all of the nutrients and vitamins you would expect.

Milk alternative is just that—an alternative to milk; in reality, a milk-flavored drink. The list of ingredients is long and hard to pronounce, it contains hydrogenated oils, and some brands even list sugar as the very first ingredient! Because milk alternatives are made from whey (a by-product of making cheese), they contain less lactose. Because of this, they don't behave the same in your cooking and baking. It is simply a drink.

HOW TO SPOT THE REAL MILK

- the ingredient list should be simple and short and list non-fat milk as the first ingredient
- can successfully be used to make yogurt or cheese, and in your baking
- stores for 20+ years, in a cool place

- the ingredient list is long and hard to pronounce, with whey or creamer as a main ingredient
- is labeled as a "milk alternative" or "milk drink"
- will fail when used to make yogurt or cheese and in some baking

How Much & What to Store

The minimum amount is enough powdered milk to make one 8-ounce glass of milk per day, per person. That glass should provide a minimum of 100 calories, 12 grams carbohydrates, 10 grams protein, and 30 grams of calcium. Keep in mind, one cup only provides one third of your RDA requirements of dairy. In addition, if your family members are big milk drinkers or you are pregnant or nursing or have small children, you probably want to double or triple the amount of powdered milk you store. Whatever you do, just be sure that you store your powdered milk in a cool area. Storing it in heat (80°F+) quickly and greatly affects the look and taste of milk products.

Find the best price.

Figuring out how much milk you need (because each company seems to have different serving sizes) and which company will offer you the best price can be quite confusing. Always check our site for up-to-date information for the best deals! *http://storethisnotthat.com/deals*

STORE THIS, NOT THAT!

 NON-INSTANT POWDERED MILK: You just can't beat the price, storage life, or the small amount of storage space they will take on your shelves.

 INSTANT POWDERED MILK: This isn't a bad option, but chances are you're overpaying for milk if you choose instant milk. But since it is still nutritional and can be used in cooking and to make yogurt or cheese, it's still a viable option.

HEADS UP: *We found that some milks that are labeled as instant in fact looked, weighed, cost, and acted like a non-instant, meaning they did not dissolve instantly in water.*

 MILK ALTERNATIVE: We're going to say no on this. Even if you are lactose intolerant, there are other shelf-stable milk alternatives (almond, rice, or soy milk) that you are probably already drinking and rotating. It may taste good, but it lacks in nutritional quality and in the ability to bake and make yogurt or cheese, and it has a short shelf-life.

DAIRY

Canned Butter

If you want real butter on your toast, then Red Feather commercially canned butter is for you. This version of butter is expensive, so it definitely falls into the luxury category and can be purchased at Emergency Essentials and online.

Shelf life: 10 years

Cost: $7–$10 per 12 oz. can.

STORE THIS!

👍 Commercially canned butter is safe to store and can be a fun treat.

👎 NEVER store "home canned" butter. The National Center for Home Food Preservation has deemed it unsafe for many reasons.

Butter Powder

Don't buy into the hype that it can be used "just like butter." It can't. It does, however, give a good, buttery flavor when used in mixes and baked goods, and it can be sprinkled on popcorn or cooked vegetables. It is also not great when used as a spread, and don't plan on melting some in your pan to sauté anything. Made from butter, milk, preservatives, and sometimes BHT.

Shelf Life: 3–5 years, 1 year opened

Average Cost: $27; 2.3 lbs.; 181 servings (1 T.); $.15 per serving; $4.82 = 1 pound fresh

How to Use: for baking, ½ cup real butter = ½ cup powder (mixed with dry ingredients) + 1½ T. water

Margarine Powder

This can be used just like the butter powder; the difference is in the ingredients. It contains the same things you find in margarine: hydrogenated soybean oil, corn syrup, additives, salt, color, and flavorings. If you prefer margarine now, then you will like this.

Shelf Life: 3–5 years, 1 year opened

Average Cost: $16; 2.2 lbs.; 176 servings (1 T.); $.09 per serving; $2.97 for 1 pound fresh

How to Use: follow directions for butter powder.

Sour Cream Powder

This product adds a tangy flavor when used as intended for baking; however, when mixed directly with water, like for a dip or topping, it is a sticky, gluey, yucky, mess. It does not look or taste like fresh sour cream. Taste test before buying—one we tried tasted more like cream cheese than sour cream. You can always use strained yogurt in place of sour cream.

Shelf Life: 5–10 years unopened; 1 year opened

Cost: Moderate, about $4 for a 'pint' of sour cream. You can use homemade yogurt to replace sour cream in baking and as fresh condiment for dips.

How to Use: It does not mix well straight into water; instead, add it with the powdered or dry part of your recipe and add the water with your other wet ingredients.

Buttermilk Powder

This is simply dried buttermilk for use in baking and cooking. It gives baked goods a tangy taste and lighter texture. Can be used for all mixes, breads, pancakes, biscuits, and cakes. Not intended for drinking. Make your own from powdered milk: Mix 1 cup milk with 2 T. vinegar, stir, and let sit 5 minutes.

Shelf life: 10–15 years   **Cost:** $20; about $7.25 for every 'quart' of buttermilk

How to Use it: Add 3 T. to every cup of water to make one cup of buttermilk, will be runny.

-LICIOUS

Cheddar Cheese Powder

This white cheese powder can be used in sauces, mixes, casseroles, pasta, rice, potato dishes, soups, breads, and popcorn. It is more expensive but by far the healthiest of the powdered cheeses, containing only cheese and salt with no milk products, starch, dyes, or corn syrup.

Find online or at Rainy Day Foods

Shelf Life: 10–15 years unopened; 1 year opened

Average Cost: $35; 3 lbs.; 51 servings (¼ cup); cost per serving: $.51.

How to Use: Make a cheese sauce mix by mixing the powder with water and heating (see recipe on can) or sprinkle on popcorn.

Cheese Blend or Cheese Powder

This bright orange powder is best known for mac and cheese but can be used in the same dishes as the cheddar cheese powder. Cheese blend is made from whey, starch, cheese blend, oil, coloring, and sometimes corn syrup (the #1 ingredient in one product). If you are a die-hard boxed mac and cheese fan or want a cheaper alternative to add a cheesy flavor to soups or sauces, this is the product for you.

Shelf Life: 10–15 years, unopened; 1 year, opened

Average Cost: $26; 3.5 lbs./57 oz.; 45 servings (¼ cup); cost per 1 cup of cheese sauce: $.59

How to Use: Best to use in a mix (see recipe on can) or sprinkle on popcorn.

Yogurt Bites

Tasty little bite-sized pieces of freeze-dried yogurt. Kids and adults love to snack on them, but can you make yogurt out of them? Are they "packed with nutrients" as one company claims, and are they cost effective? Yes, you can make yogurt, although at $15 per cup it is very expensive. (Learn how to make your own yogurt for cheaper, page 108.) The bites are made from sugar, fruit purée, skim yogurt, tapioca starch, and flavor, and except for a very small amount of vitamins from the fruit, the only other ingredients mentioned are sugars and carbs, so we would say NO to the health claims.

Average Cost: $43; as a snack, $1.25 for ¼ cup serving; as yogurt $11.25 for 6 oz.

Shelf Life: 3–5 years; 3 months opened

How to use: eat dry (drink lots of water); or add ¼ cup water to 3 cups bites to make ¾ cup yogurt.

👎 NOT THAT!

Yogurt bites contain about double the calories and triple the sugar of ice cream. In our opinion, this "yogurt" should be considered an expensive dessert and eaten sparingly.

Freeze-Dried Cheese

This is real shredded cheese. When hydrated, use it as you would fresh cheese to make gooey grilled cheese sandwiches or as a topping on pizza. It is fairly expensive but a fun treat.

Shelf Life: 10–15 years unopened, 1 year opened

Average Cost: $39 or $15 for a 'pound' or four cups of shredded cheese; $1.88 for 1 cup cheese sauce.

Varieties: Mozzarella, Colby, Cheddar, Monterey Jack, Sharp Cheddar

How to use it: To hydrate, put desired amount in a bowl then lightly sprinkle or spray with cold water, a little at a time. Using a fork, toss cheese and water together, letting it soak in as you go, just until there is a little water in the bottom of the bowl. Allow cheese to sit until all liquid is absorbed. If possible, cover and let sit in refrigerator overnight. Always reconstitute cheese before using or it won't melt correctly.

Shelf-Stable Whipping Cream & Half-and-Half

Whipping Cream or Half-and-Half in a box. That's right, real liquid, shelf-stable cream that come in cup- and pint-sized packing and have a 1–2 year shelf life. Just chill and use as fresh. Made by Gossner and Hershey, this can be found in some grocery stores, Honeyville locations, or online. Great deal at $1 per 8 oz.

👍 STORE THIS!

AN Egg-cellent CHOICE

Eggs are full of protein, a necessity in baking, and perfect for your food storage.

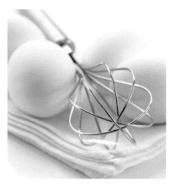

AN EGG-CELLENT CHOICE FOR BAKING: WHOLE EGG POWDER

Powdered eggs are one of food storage's best kept secrets! They are already pasteurized, which means no threat of salmonella poisoning, and they can be stored at room temperature. They are also easy and safe for children to use—no messy eggshells to dig out. They are great to use in baked goods but are a poor substitute for fresh eggs for breakfast as they make disgusting (it's the brutal truth) scrambled eggs or omelets.

Shelf Life: 3–5 years unopened; 1 year opened
Cost: Usually 1–2 times the price of fresh eggs.
How to use them: Whole eggs and water have a 1:2 ratio. One egg = 1 T. dry powdered egg white + 2 tsp. water (if you're using them in a cake you may need to double the amounts for one egg). Add powder to dry ingredients and water to wet ingredients.

AN EGG-CELLENT CHOICE FOR EGG WHITES: POWDERED EGG WHITES

Powdered egg whites are most certainly the coolest thing since sliced bread. This is actually what large bakeries use to make angel food cakes, meringues, and any other baked good that requires whipped egg whites! Yes, that is correct, you'll never have to spend time separating the egg white from the egg yolk again. Powdered egg whites are the no-fail method for perfectly whipped egg whites EVERY TIME. Plus, if you're watching your cholesterol intake, this is a much cheaper option than buying the liquid form of egg whites from your local grocery store.

Shelf Life: 3–5 years unopened; 1 year opened
Cost: Usually cheaper than store bought egg whites.
How to use them: Powdered egg whites and water have a 1:3 ratio. One egg white = 1 T. dry powdered egg white + 3 tsp. water. If whipping, combine water and powder and whip until desired texture is achieved. For baking, add powder to dry ingredients and water to the wet ingredients.

AN EGG-CELLENT CHOICE FOR BREAKFAST EGGS: OVA-EASY EGG CRYSTALS

These should not be confused with a generic scrambled egg mix, which is terrible for making scrambled eggs. Conversely, these are great to use for making scrambled eggs, omelets, and anything that requires fresh eggs. OvaEasy has all the benefits of a dried egg powder but with a natural fresh taste. It is made with a revolutionary process that gently extracts water while preserving the delicious flavor and nutritional benefits of fresh eggs. These are not as cheap as the whole egg powder or as fresh eggs, but unless you plan on raising chickens—this is the best way to have eggs for breakfast. These also come in egg white crystals.

Shelf Life: 7 years unopened; 1 year opened
Cost: Usually 3–4 times the price of fresh eggs.
How to use them: 2 tsp. of the egg crystals + 3 T. of water = 1 egg
Simply add water to these egg crystals and you're ready to cook or scramble.

Do you have an egg allergy? Then you'll want to store unflavored gelatin (like the Knox brand) to use in place of eggs.

Fruits & Vegetables

GETTING THE MOST FOR YOUR MONEY

When considering cost and storage space, there really is a big difference between products. Let's look, for example, at the cost and number of cans it actually takes to make 100 half-servings of peas.

Dehydrated: 1 #10 can, weighs 4 pounds, costs $28

Canned: 28 (15-oz.) cans, weighs 28 lbs, costs $28

Freeze-dried: 5 #10 cans, weighs 5 pounds, costs $95

EAT YOUR FRUIT AND VEGGIES!

A phrase commonly heard by most kids growing up. Why? Because our mothers inherently knew that fruits and vegetables would help us grow up big and strong. They contain vitamins, enzymes, and nutrients and have other amazing properties that help our bodies to heal, help prevent diseases, and aid in digestion.

That's all well and good, but do you know why we like them so much? They add so much color, texture, and variety to a meal. Can you imagine a world without apples and cinnamon in your oatmeal or vegetables in your stew? We can't either, and that is why, after you get your basic food storage, you are going to want to add fruits and vegetables. This is your chance to add color, taste, and variety to your meals.

COMPARE APPLES TO APPLES

We found that comparing product prices between food storage companies was challenging because of the differences in serving sizes in their #10 cans. For some reason, instead of using a uniform serving size, like the canned food industry does (½ cup), they like to mix it up. We found serving sizes that ranged from 2 teaspoons up to one cup! So confusing! So, to make things easier for all of us, we converted the products into ½-cup serving sizes. This made it possible to really compare. Oh, you want to know this too? Go to our website, where we share up-to-date information.

BUYER BEWARE

Freeze-dried fruits and vegetables are big money makers for the food storage companies. They want you to believe that they are cheaper and easier and therefore better than using fresh

or canned, so you should use them every day. Wrong! With few exceptions, freeze-dried is by far the most expensive way to store food, averaging 5x more expensive than other options.

CANNED, BOTTLED, OR DRIED—WHICH SHOULD YOU PICK?

Whether the fruits or vegetables are canned, bottled, dried, dehydrated, or freeze-dried, they have been picked at the peak of ripeness, when they are the sweetest, then washed and trimmed to leave only the best parts, and then processed immediately, preserving the majority of their precious nutrients. There are, however, big differences in the taste and quality of non-fresh fruits and vegetables. In our testing we found that some tasted better canned, some dried or dehydrated, and some freeze-dried. If you don't know the difference between dried, dehydrated, and freeze-dried, you are not alone. We have sprinkled that information throughout the fruit and vegetable pages, so by the end of this you will be experts on these shelf-stable foods. Bottom line, to get what you really want you will probably want a combination of canned, bottled, and dried varieties.

 Find the best price.

Stay up-to-date with the current fruit and vegetable pricing and deals. *http://storethisnotthat.com/deals*

Fruit
ANY WAY YOU SLICE IT

Why store fruits, you ask? That's easy. Who doesn't love apple-cinnamon oatmeal or berry pie? Fruits are processed in a variety of ways and come in different kinds of packaging, all of which bring sweetness and joy to our short- and long-term food storage. These fruits make tasty snacks and can used in cereals, breads, spreads, syrups, and desserts! Before we get down to our Store This, Not That list, there are some "berry" important things you should know about fruit.

What kind of fruits should you pick? Whatever varieties your family likes. With almost 20 kinds available, there is something for everyone. Keep in mind, the bigger the variety the better. Why? Because different colored fruits contain different kinds of vitamins and minerals to keep you healthy and strong. How can I store fruit long-term? You can buy it canned, dried, dehydrated, or freeze-dried, and of course bottle it fresh from the garden. Packaged fruit, if kept in a cool, dark place, will store for many, many years.

SHATTERING THE MYTHS OF CANNED AND BOTTLED FOOD

Did you know that canned fruits and vegetables have as much, and in some cases more, fiber, vitamins, and minerals than their fresh counterparts? Foods that have been properly processed and sealed up in an airtight

can or bottle are safe and edible long after the processing time—over one hundred years, according to studies. Of course the look, taste, and nutrition deteriorate over time, but it is still safe to eat for years after the "best by" date. For optimum taste and nutrition, store in a cool, dark place, eat within 5 years, and always discard any leaking or bulging cans. Overall, the texture and taste of canned fruit is closer to fresh than either reconstituted dehydrated or freeze-dried fruit, although it is lower in vitamins A and C. Make sure you rotate cans with pull tops and tomato products regularly so they don't leak.

 DON'T STORE CHEAP FOOD BRANDS: They are much more likely to leak and usually have less food product with more liquid. Refer back to our "Secrets to Grocery Store Shopping" section to find out when name-brand fruits and vegetables are on sale.

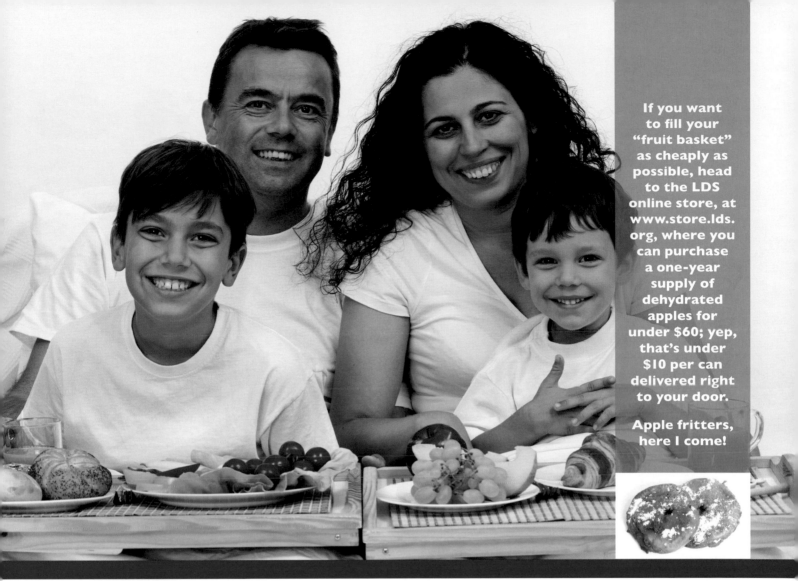

DRIED FRUIT

Dried fruits (the soft kind you buy at the store) are sweeter and chewier than canned or freeze-dried fruit. They contain more moisture than commercially dehydrated fruits and so are soft and pliable; because of this, they have a short shelf life (6–12 months). Your family probably already eats dried fruits. Raisins, craisins, mango, figs, prunes, and others fall into this category. Dried fruits are delicious, but to avoid spoilage, only buy what your family eats so you can rotate it frequently.

DEHYDRATED FRUIT

Commercially dehydrated (DH) fruits (and veggies) are very dry, hard, and usually wrinkled in appearance. They are smaller than when they were fresh, and for this reason they take up much less space than either canned or freeze-dried product. Apples and bananas can be munched on dry but other fruits or veggies will be too hard until rehydrated. DH foods take a bit longer to rehydrate than freeze-dried but they will return to full size and not be mushy. Commercial varieties include: apples, applesauce, banana chips, peaches, and raisins. Storage life: 10 years (keep in cool place). When dehydrating at home, almost any fruit will work, and it is as sweet as candy; yum! Stores 2 years if packaged airtight.

FREEZE-DRIED FRUIT

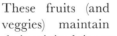

These fruits (and veggies) maintain their original size and shape and have a light, airy, crunchy texture. Because of their airy nature, they rehydrate very quickly, unlike dried or dehydrated foods. Freeze-dried fruits and vegetables look inviting and some are even pretty good when popped directly in your mouth, although, in our opinion, a few taste a lot like flavored styrofoam. Generally, with the exception of berries and a few veggies, freeze-dried products have less flavor than their canned or dehydrated counterparts, and they are rather mushy when reconstituted. Storage life: up to 25 years or 1 year after opening if kept away from moisture.

Warning: When munching on dehydrated or freeze-dried fruits, drink LOTS of water. Eating more than a handful of dry fruits all at one time may cause you to feel somewhat sick and clogged up.

Fruit
KNOW-HOW

HOW MANY BUSHELS WILL YOU NEED?

Now that is a good question. The USDA says 5–13 servings of fruits and vegetables per day, but studies show as little as one-half cup serving per day or even less will suffice.

So for one year, ½ cup per day breaks down to: 104 cans, 45 quarts, or 16 #10 cans per person, which is still a lot of food to store, a lot of expense, and very overwhelming!

If you have unlimited money, are great at rotating, and have the storage space, go for it!

But if you are like us, you need a more doable plan, a more realistic one, so when life takes a twist, you can supplement what you have stored with what you can grow or buy. If, however, your complete survival depends on what you have stored, fruits will be a luxury, not a staple, which is why growing your own berries and fruit is so important. Here is our suggestion.

MIXING IT UP . . . YOUR FRUIT GOAL

A mixture of the following should meet your basic needs per person.

 OR   OR

25 quarts bottled

50 15-oz. cans

8 #10 cans dehydrated or freeze-dried

ARE THE CLAIMS TRUE?

For the most part, freeze-dried and dehydrated fruit does not look or taste like fresh no matter what anyone says. It is best used to make something or snacked on dry (drink LOTS of water) and not rehydrated and eaten as a bowl of fruit.

THE LAW OF REHYDRATING

Most rehydrating instructions are ridiculous! Dehydrated fruits do need to sit in room temperature water for a time to fully rehydrate; however, freeze-dried fruits should never be rehydrated in hot or warm water and never be mixed with more than a 1:1 ratio of water to fruit, let alone a 3:1 ratio, unless you want a tasteless mass of mush when you are done.

FREEZE-DRIED FOODS ARE ALREADY FULL SIZE, SO THEY DO NOT EXPAND WHEN REHYDRATED.

DEHYDRATED FOODS WILL DOUBLE OR TRIPLE IN SIZE AFTER REHYDRATING.

TRY IT FIRST

Dehydrated and freeze-dried fruits come in a variety of tastes, shapes, sizes, and quality, but most products are similar, apples to apples, etc. To make sure you like it BEFORE you buy, try a sample. Most of the companies will let you do this in their stores, or you can order a sample pack from Rainy Day Foods. To get your money's worth, never buy the small cans.

Get to Know
YOUR FRUIT OPTIONS

	FREEZE-DRIED	DEHYDRATED	DRIED	CANNED	BEST BUY
APPLE SLICES	✓	✓			dehydrated
APPLESAUCE		✓		✓	canned
APRICOT	✓	✓	✓	✓	dried
BANANA	✓	✓			either
BLACKBERRY	✓			✓	neither
BLUEBERRY	✓	✓	✓	✓	freeze-dried
CHERRY	✓		✓		dried
CRANBERRIES	✓		✓	✓	dried/canned
GRAPES	✓	✓	✓		dried
MANGO	✓		✓	✓	dried
ORANGE	✓			✓	canned
PEACH	✓			✓	canned
PEAR	✓			✓	canned
PINEAPPLE	✓		✓	✓	canned
RASPBERRY	✓			✓	freeze-dried
STRAWBERRY	✓		✓	✓	freeze-dried

GARDEN FRUITS & TREES

Never discount what you can grow at home in your garden or on trees to supplement your storage! Melons are delicious and juicy and can grow in almost any garden!

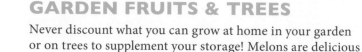 # STORE THIS

Love it? Get it! Don't let fruit-buying decisions bog you down—just buy what your family will eat. It never saves money to throw food away. Here are our best tips to make the buying easier.

FRUIT SPREADS

are a great addition to any food storage because they taste like real fruit and double as a topping for breads.

FREEZE-DRIED BERRIES

are delicious as a snack, in cereals, or in desserts. Plus, when berries are not in season, the freeze-dried varieties can actually save you money!

FREEZE-DRIED BERRIES, namely strawberries, raspberries, and blueberries, taste very similar to fresh. Added bonus: for most of the year, when berries aren't on sale, they can actually be cheaper than fresh! Be sure and follow our rehydrating hints found on p. 70 for freshest taste.

FREEZE-DRIED MANGOS are a fan favorite. They are mildly mango-flavored and have a delicious tart taste, great for snacking.

DEHYDRATED FRUITS are crunchy and full of flavor! We love dehydrated apple slices (great for snacking and pie!) and banana chips (people either love them or hate them—so you choose). Most fruits can be dehydrated at home.

CANNED FRUIT can be a great option. The varieties packed in juice taste freshest and you can drink the juice (a fun treat!). The fruit is firm, juicy, and up to 80% cheaper than freeze-dried fruit. Our favorite choices are peaches, pears, fruit cocktail, mandarin oranges, pineapple, applesauce, and cranberry sauce.

DRIED FRUIT can be a great addition for snacking or in cereals. They pack a punch of flavor and have a great chewy texture. But be careful, some of them have added sugar! Varieties we love dried are cherries, raisins, apricots, mangos, and craisins.

CANNED FRUIT

tastes more like real fruit because they are firm and juicy. Added bonus: they are a fraction of the price of freeze-dried fruit!

DO-IT-YOURSELF

A lot of fruits, not offered in stores, can be home dehydrated! Check out our special DIY section for more information!

FREEZE-DRIED GRAPES

Grapes are yummy because they are crisp and juicy and pop in your mouth. Freeze-dried grapes are none of those.

👎 NOT THAT

There are some great fruit choices available for storage, but in our opinion, these are not them. They did not meet our taste or quality standards. As always, try it. If you like it, store it anyway.

FREEZE-DRIED PEACHES & PEARS

are expensive, bland, and fragile (turn into powder), and when rehydrated they are mushy. If you really want peaches or pears, consider canned, home dehydrated, or one of our favorites—JAM!

FREEZE-DRIED APPLES

are bland and fragile. They aren't good for snacking or in pie or other dishes because they get mushy. The FD Fuji and Granny Smith varieties have more flavor, but are irregular sizes and have tough skins attached, which are unappetizing and hard to use for baking. Stick with DH apples slices.

CANNED BERRIES

are mushy blobs of fruit floating in sugar syrup. Why settle for these when you can have the great tasting freeze-dried alternatives or jam?

FREEZE-DRIED BERRIES GONE BAD.

FD Cranberries are sour and best for sauce. So just store the canned sauce. FD Cherries are not good and very expensive. If you want cherries, store dried ones. FD Blackberries made our worst list. They can best be described as crunchy seeds covered in a thin coating of bitterness. Yuck! Grow your own or make jam!

FREEZE-DRIED GRAPES AND ORANGES

aren't sweet or juicy. Instead, they are dry and crunchy with very mild flavor. Plus, the grapes taste somewhat like raisins and can only be used for snacking. And the oranges are SO expensive! If you really want oranges, store canned. If you want grapes, store raisins—they are more versatile and can be used for baking and snacking.

FREEZE-DRIED ORANGES

People don't usually crave dry crisp oranges—you know?

FREEZE-DRIED BANANAS

People either love them or hate them, but please don't use them every day in smoothies unless it's an emergency. They cost 8x more than fresh bananas!

FREEZE-DRIED PEACHES & PEARS

Freeze-dried peaches, pears, and apples can be very bland and have a texture similar to styrofoam. Plus, they can cost 4x more than your other options.

CANNED BERRIES

Canned berries are usually packed in heavy syrup and are expensive!

Vegetables
ANY WAY YOU SLICE IT

Vegetables can turn chicken and gravy into a scrumptious pot pie or bouillon into a mouth-watering soup, and then there are the dishes where they are the featured star, like in pumpkin pie! Let's face it, without vegetables our main meals would be devoid of color and variety. Veggies also lend a hand in the area of taste and texture too! If you didn't before, you can now see how truly valuable vegetables are and will be in making delicious meals from basic food storage—and don't even get us started on what you can do with potatoes: yum!

What kinds of vegetables do you use right now? Our guess would be, probably mostly fresh or frozen with a few cans of corn thrown in, right? Great, that is a good place to begin, but unless you are growing all of them yourself, and are bottling up the extras year round, you may want to have a back-up plan, and that is where we come in. We have tried and tasted the shelf-stable vegetable products available out there, and we can't wait to share our observations with you. So sit down, relax, and prepare to find out which vegetables will be the most valuable to your family's storage.

SOMEWHERE IN THE RAINBOW ARE THE PERFECT VEGGIES FOR YOU!

Fresh and shelf-stable vegetables come in a rainbow of colors, everything from red to purple and even black and white! For the most part, the brighter the color of the vegetable, the healthier it is, and they are all out there waiting for you to find them and add them to your food storage. Whether you decide on canned, home bottled, dehydrated, or freeze-dried, the nutrition is close to the same. So what do you do? Make a list of the vegetables that your family already likes and uses in your meals. Don't forget things like onions, celery, carrots, and peppers that are the flavor foundation in many dishes, and then let us guide you to the best ones for your family's shelf and lifestyle.

Weighing out your options: Dried fruits and vegetables (meaning dehydrated and freeze-dried) are more—sometimes much more—expensive than canned, but they do have a longer shelf life, and they take up far less room. So if you know it's something you are not going to rotate or just don't have the room for, and it is an important ingredient to your meals, spending the extra money may be the best option for your family.

THE TRUTH ABOUT TOMATOES

Tomatoes are a staple in our houses. They are beautiful and tasty, and we love to eat them in soup, salsa, and marinara. We especially love them fresh from the garden; however, we cannot always get them that way. That is why we are so grateful that there are so many shelf-stable tomato options available. You can buy them canned, bottle them, dehydrate them to use sliced, or grind them into powder (see our DIY section) or buy them already powdered under the fancy name of "tomato powder." Canned tomatoes are juicy, easy to use, and so full of flavor. They are a top pick. But we also love using tomato powder. Just adding a few tablespoons to soups or stews will give it a big punch of flavor. In fact, one heaping tablespoon of tomato powder adds as much flavor as a whole pint of canned tomatoes! You can also just add water to the powder and make tomato sauce, juice, paste, or even pizza sauce! Take it from us; a can of tomato powder will go a long way!

ROTTEN TOMATOES: Steer clear of freeze-dried tomatoes. Unlike fresh or canned tomatoes, they have more of a mild, sun-dried tomato flavor, and the cost is, well, rotten. About 7x more than canned tomatoes!

SUPER SPUDS

Dehydrated potatoes, in all their varieties, are one of the best-kept secrets in the culinary world. They come already sliced, diced, shredded, mashed and flaked—great for everyday cooking or long term storage. You may have seen them on your grocery store shelves in scalloped and au gratin potatoes and soup mixes, but did you know that many restaurants are using them for mashed potatoes and even hash browns? If they are using them, why aren't you? Most forms of dehydrated potatoes double in size when cooking. They can be used in mashed potatoes, bread, potato cakes, omelets, dips, soups, hashbrowns, casseroles, and even desserts! What a great, inexpensive way to add variety to your food storage!

LABEL ALERT . . . Flakes vs. Mashed: Use your label reading skills to discover whether the "mashed" potatoes you are buying are complete mashed potatoes or just flakes. Potato flakes are just light flakes of cooked, flattened potatoes, usually used for thickener or in bread dough. But "mashed" potatoes (called gems, beads, pearls, or mashed) usually include milk, salt, and flavoring, thus just needing boiling water for creamy, buttery mashed potatoes. Flakes store 20 years versus "mashed" that only store about 3 years.

Veggie

KNOW-HOW

See our DIY section for more information on sprouting.

YOUR VEGGIE GOAL

Choosing the vegetables you want to store is as easy as pie; just pick a variety of kinds you like. Optimally, you will have some vegetables growing in a garden, some in cans or bottles, and others dehydrated or freeze-dried.

If you are like us, you need a doable plan that covers the basics and allows you to add to it when the money is available. Here is our suggestion of what to plan for when storing vegetables.

A mixture of the following should meet your basic needs per person.

25 OR **50** OR **8**

quarts bottled | 15-oz. cans | #10 cans dehydrated or freeze-dried

GETTING THE BIGGEST BANG FOR YOUR BUCK

However, if you want a more specific basic plan (per person) that will give you the biggest bang for your buck and should allow you to make basic soups, stews, etc.—we suggest starting your vegetable collection this way.

| half #10 can of DH onions | half #10 can of DH celery | half #10 can of DH carrots | half #10 can of tomato powder | 25 wet pack cans tomatoes | six #10 cans of your choice |

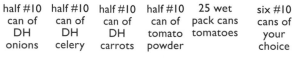

Bonus three #10 cans potatoes: diced, sliced, shredded, mashed, or flakes

VEGGIES IN A BOTTLE

Sprouting is a great way to grow vegetables year round in very little space. Sprouts add fresh, live food to what could be a very dull diet. Vegetable sprouts include broccoli, cabbage, lettuce, radish, peas, and alfalfa, which probably isn't technically a vegetable, but it is green so we think it should count.

FRESHER VEGGIES

If you want a fresher taste and texture for your dehydrated carrots, or freeze-dried corn, green beans, or peas, simply cover them with warm water, let them sit on the counter for 10 minutes, then put them in the refrigerator for a few hours or overnight. This method added pop to our corn and peas, crunch to the carrots (DH), and tenderized the green beans. It did not have any beneficial effect on any other vegetables.

THE LAW OF REHYDRATING

As with the fruits, the rehydrating instructions on the labels are utterly unreliable. Generally, most vegetables will be used in soups or other dishes containing liquid.

In this case, the vegetables can be added to the dish dry, where it will rehydrate as it cooks, adding in extra water as needed.

If you are using them as a side dish, or in something that has little liquid, you will need to rehydrate them first.

Dehydrated vegetables (and fruits) are at their best when rehydrated in double the amount of liquid overnight in the refrigerator. They can also be simmered in boiling water for 10–22 minutes and then drained.

Freeze-dried vegetables, on the other hand, are at their best when just barely covered in hot water for 3–10 minutes and then drained.

Get to Know
YOUR VEGETABLE OPTIONS

	VARIETIES	FREEZE-DRIED	DEHYDRATED	CANNED	BEST-BUY
ASPARAGUS		✓		✓	taste test first
BELL PEPPERS	diced & sliced	✓	✓		dehydrated
BROCCOLI		✓			freeze-dried
BUTTERNUT SQUASH		✓			garden
CABBAGE			✓	✓	dehydrated
CARROTS	sliced, diced, shredded	✓	✓	✓	dehydrated
CAULIFLOWER		✓			freeze-dried
CELERY		✓	✓		dehydrated
CORN		✓	✓	✓	canned or freeze-dried
GREEN CHILES		✓		✓	canned
GREEN BEANS		✓	✓	✓	canned or freeze-dried
GREEN ONIONS		✓			freeze-dried or garden
MIXED VEGGIES		✓		✓	canned
MUSHROOMS		✓	✓		dehydrated or canned
OLIVES	sliced & whole	✓		✓	canned
ONIONS		✓	✓		dehydrated
PEAS		✓	✓	✓	canned or freeze-dried
POTATOES	pearls, mashed, diced, shreds,	✓	✓	✓	dehydrated
SWEET POTATOES		✓		✓	canned
ZUCCHINI		✓			garden

DIY GARDEN VEGGIES

Zucchini, tomatoes, and more grow in any garden, very plentifully. What a great way to supplement your food storage! Check out our DIY section for more information.

👍 STORE THIS

There were lots of vegetables to taste, and surprisingly our top picks did so well we would feel good about having them as a side dish at dinner, and that is saying a lot! Others would be good cooked in soups, sauces, and main dishes. Some even made the "eat them dry like candy" list.

SALSA & SAUCES
Salsa and spaghetti sauce are a great source of vegetables!

FREEZE-DRIED BROCCOLI
Tastes great, looks and feels like fresh, and canned is not an option. It's so good it could be a standalone side dish!

TOP PICKS: Freeze-dried broccoli, cauliflower, corn, green beans, and peas are easy to rehydrate and they look and taste almost like fresh! We can see using them in main dishes or even as a standalone side dish. The peas and corn are so sweet you can just pop them in your mouth as a quick snack.

CANNED VEGETABLES
If you love them, use them. They are packed in liquid which can be used for the liquid in your recipe. Best choices for canned include corn, green chiles, mushrooms, olives, sauerkraut, and tomatoes. Asparagus, peas, and green beans are good options if you like their texture.

DEHYDRATED POTATOES
Potatoes are a comfort food, and with so many varieties to choose from, you can make all your family favorites—from skillet scrambles to soups.

DEHYDRATED SPINACH AND SLICED MUSHROOMS (found at Rainy Day Foods) are both surprisingly good. After soaking just a few minutes, they looked and tasted like fresh. These would be a great addition to pizza, sauces, or main dishes.

DEHYDRATED CARROTS, once rehydrated, offer all the taste and benefits of fresh carrots. They are brightly colored, sweet and crunchy. They are available diced, sliced (Emergency Essentials), and even shredded (Honeyville). They are great for snacking, soups, and even on a salad.

AROMATIC VEGETABLES
Celery, carrots, bell peppers, and onions are the aromatic vegetables that make the base for any great soup or sauce. Dehydrated versions (found at Rainy Day Foods) will give you twice as many servings per can!

CANNED VEGGIES
Store the canned vegetables your family already eats. Remember, variety is the spice of life.

ZE-DRIED OLIVES

...amily likes the canned variety, then don't ...extra money on the freeze-dried variety.

OT THAT

...at vegetables available, but in our ...e the naughty list, the don't-ever- ...his list. Want to know what those ...t you would, so here is our most excellent advice.

GOURMET VEGETABLES

It's always important to ask yourself if it is a "want" or a "need." Get the basics first—your wallet will thank you!

FREEZE-DRIED TOMATO DICES

Remember, these cost 8x more than canned tomatoes and have a sun-dried tomato flavor.

"FREEZE-DRIED" MIXED VEGETABLES

These are actually a combination of freeze-dried and dehydrated vegetables. The peas and corn are freeze-dried and the carrots are dehydrated. Mixing dehydrated and freeze-dried vegetables together can make rehydrating and cooking really tricky since they each take different amounts of time to cook.

MIXED VEGETABLES

We love this idea, but they mix dehydrated vegetables with freeze-dried, and that gets you overcooked freeze-dried vegetables and undercooked dehydrated.

FREEZE-DRIED SQUASH

In our testing, we found that neither of the freeze-dried butternut or zucchini had much flavor and both, when rehydrated, had texture similar to a sponge.

FREEZE-DRIED POTATO DICES

Not only are these more fragile and cost a lot more than dehydrated options, they also taste like mashed potato globules.

MEET THE MEATS

Where's the beef? This phrase got us thinking . . . if we wanted to have beef in our beef stew or bacon with our eggs, could we? What kinds of beef, chicken, fish, and other shelf-stable meats are available in the 21st century, and are there any meat alternatives? Much to our surprise, we found over 20 different varieties of meats and meat substitutes. We gathered, opened, (prepared, if necessary), and consumed these dried, freeze-dried (FD), canned, and bottled meats so we could compare their appearance, price, taste, and textures and share our discoveries with you! (You can thank us later.) We found that some were real meat and some were not. Some were tender, juicy, and full of flavor, while others not so much. Some were a good value but others were really not! You may not be able to sit down to a traditional turkey dinner using shelf-stable meats, but you'll definitely be able to recreate the taste and smell of it! And to answer our question, yes, there are some great options for beef and bacon. To help you find the "Best of the Best" in the meat category, let's go **MEET the MEATS.**

meat secrets as easy as 1-2-3

1. understand the differences

There are three basic choices for storing meats: freeze-dried, canned, and bottled. Freeze-dried (FD) meat is real, cooked meat that has been quickly frozen and dried. After it is rehydrated in boiling water for a few minutes, it is pretty close to fresh. Commercially, canned meats (metal cans) and home bottled (in glass jars) are two other methods that are also real meat. The meat is put in a can or jar and pressure canned with high heat. When cooking, it produces its own broth and comes out tender and flaky. Both the freeze-dried and the canned meats look, taste, feel like, and can be used as cooked meat. Texturized Vegetable Protein (TVP), on the other hand, are meat-flavored nuggets made from soy flour, soybean oil, and salt that sometimes contain sugar, corn syrup, and yeast. They are advertised as meat substitutes, but they don't look, smell, or taste anything like real meat.

2. meat math

Most of us know what a pound of bacon or hamburger looks like and what a good price per pound is, right? But how does that compare to meat that is already cooked and packaged in a #10 can, 12-ounce can, or pint-sized jar? The simplified answer is this, on average:

A) 1 #10 can FD meat = 22 ½-cup servings = 5.5 pounds fresh meat (2 cups per pound)

B) 2 12-oz. cans meat = 4 ½-cup servings = 1 pound fresh meat

C) 1 pint home bottled = 4 ½-cup servings = 1 pound fresh meat

D) 1 #10 can TVP = 4 ¼-cup servings (makes 4½ cups) = 5 pounds fresh meat

There can be big differences in FD meat pricing between companies, so shop around for best deals. On average, FD meat is 2x more expensive than canned and canned is 2x more expensive than home canning.

3. know when to use it

Canned and home-bottled meats are great for 90-day supply menus and for use in everyday meals when you are out of fresh meat or short on time. However, make no bones about it, using FD meat on a daily basis is NOT going to save you money no matter what you hear online or at a food storage party. It is best stored and saved for when meat isn't available or affordable, and only if you can afford to replace it. Last and least, in our opinion, is TVP. It does not look or taste anything like real meat. Some think it is okay when eaten dry, which works if you want to snack on "meat-ish"-flavored, dog food–looking nuggets, but doesn't help much if you want to use it in main dishes. It can be used as a meat extender (check the FD meatball label or the label of any frozen meatball sold at your local grocer) mixed in with other fresh meat. But used on its own, it's soggy and gross. You probably can see that we aren't big fans of TVP, but there are many who really like it, so once again . . . if you like it, buy it.

Check out our **Thanksgiving Casserole** recipe on page 116

CANNED MEAT

Varieties: 8 different kinds (see chart).
Average Price: $7 per pound.
Storage Life: 3–5 years; store in cool area for best taste.
Pros: Open and eat, contains broth that can replace liquids in recipes; cans don't break; can be purchased at local stores.
Cons: meat has slight metal taste; twice the price and heavier than freeze-dried.

Varieties: 10 different kinds (see chart).
Average Price: $12 per pound.
Storage Life: 10–15 years, if stored in conditions under 70 degrees.
Pros: Long storage life, easy to use, just soak or add directly to soups; lightweight; most had close to fresh taste and appearance.

FREEZE-DRIED MEAT

Cons: Expensive; once opened, use within 2 weeks or repackage in airtight container; some varieties crumble or have a dry or unpleasant taste; store extra water for use.

TEXTURIZED VEGETABLE PROTEIN

Varieties: bacon, beef, chicken, ham, sausage, sloppy joe, taco.
Average Price: $1.30 = 1 pound meat.
Storage Life: 10 years, if cool.
Pros: Vegetarian, high protein, cheap.
Cons: bland when rehydrated; sloppy joe and taco had very odd tastes; all had sponge-like texture which continued to expand when sitting in liquid. Don't be surprised if it gives you tummy trouble.

Varieties: beef, chicken, pork, rabbit, seafood, and turkey.
Average Price: $.85 ($0 if you have jar and lid) plus cost of one pound of meat.
Storage Life: 2–5 years for best taste, store in cool area.
Pros: open and eat; contains broth for use in recipe; by far the cheapest way to store meat; simple to can (need pressure canner); can personalize meats (fajita, BBQ pork, etc.).
Cons: need pressure canner; jars breakable; heavy and bulky to store.

HOME BOTTLED MEAT

« MEAT IS NEAT »

FILLING UP YOUR MEAT LOCKER

HOW MUCH DO YOU NEED?

You don't really need any meat because your protein needs will be met with your grains and beans, so it is really a question of how much you want. Our recommendation is ¼ cup per person, per day, increasing as desired. So what does that look like? A combination of the following:

90
12-oz. cans

OR

45
pints bottled

OR

8
#10 cans freeze-dried

BACON OR BUST

Guess what, you can have your bacon and eat it too! It can be expensive, but it is available. (Most need to be refrigerated after opening.) There are several options for real, good-tasting, safe-to-eat, shelf-stable bacon/bits:

 1  2  3

Real bacon bits in a JAR by Hormel

Real bacon bits in a BAG by Hormel, Oscar Meyer, or Kirkland

Real bacon strips in a CAN by Yoder, 50 strips (found on the web)

OR BUST: We know, home canning your own bacon sounds like such a good idea, and we thought so too. However, there is danger of botulism when doing this. Unfortunately, no testing verifies that home canning is safe.

PEPPERONI PIZZA ANYONE?

Are you dreaming of a pepperoni-covered pizza? Then shelf-stable pepperoni is the product for you. It is available at local stores either on a rack or shelf or in the cooler by cheeses. It will say "refrigerate after opening" in small print. This is your clue that it is shelf-stable until opened. To top off the good news, it tastes good! For best taste, stores up to 2 years.

SEPARATING THE MEAT FROM THE BONE

Just think of us like your neighborhood butcher: helpful, friendly, picking the best cuts of meat, steering you away from the bad, and trimming away the fat before sending you on your way. We made our decisions based on look, taste, texture, and price—obviously, if you like it, then buy it.

👍 STORE THIS

Freeze Dried	sausage, ham (small dice), turkey, beef
Canned	beef, chicken, bacon/bits, ham/spam
Bottled	all meats (customized flavors and cheap)
Dried	pepperoni, bacon/bits
Dehydrated	ground beef (DIY), shrimp

👎 NOT THAT

Freeze Dried	chicken and ground beef (dry & very fragile), ham (large dice, chewy) mini meatballs (bad taste and ingredients)
Bottled	ham, bacon
TVP	ALL
Dehydrated	drying canned meats (expensive)

BUY BIG AND SAVE WITH ZAYCON FRESH

Zaycon Fresh is a company that offers you the opportunity to buy high-quality, much-fresher-than-the-store beef, chicken, pork, ribs, fish, and more. We love to buy their meats! Sometimes we keep it all for ourselves and eat some fresh, freeze some, and then pressure can the rest (this is SO EASY— see our DIY section). Other times we ask friends or family to split the cases with us.

Any way you slice it, it's so easy. Just order, pay online, pick up product from the truck, and take home and enjoy. Follow the link on storethisnotthat.com to sign up and see what products are coming to your area.

HAM IT UP

Does your family love scalloped potatoes, split pea soup, or breakfast burritos with ham? Are you feeling sad because the expensive freeze-dried ham is out of your price range? Then we have some suggestions that should turn that frown upside down.

(oval shaped, 1-lb. size) found at grocery and drug stores, about $3

(6-oz. can) found in grocery stores, about $3

Spam (an old favorite, 12-oz. tin), about $4

FISH FRY?

We couldn't find any substitutes to use for fried fish, but there are lots of choices to get your fish fix. There are, of course, canned creatures such as herring, mackerel, mussels, sardines, salmon, and tuna to whet your palate. But did you know that many ethnic grocery stores also carry dried fish and even shrimp? Just think of it, you could turn plain rice into shrimp-fried rice. Yum!

DEHYDRATE
YOUR OWN MEAT

If you thought, like we did, that dehydrating meat that is shelf-stable was an urban legend, then you would be wrong! Of course, we know that you can make jerky, but everything we read said that it would only store safely at room temperatures for a couple of weeks. That doesn't do us much good if we are trying to add to our food storage. After combing the USDA and National Center for Home Food Preservation (NCHFP) and further communication with them, we are now happy to report that if you follow the guidelines, you can dehydrate and store meat at room temperatures for one year and beyond. This includes fresh lean meat such as beef, hamburger, chicken, some fish, and all canned meats. By following specific guidelines for drying and storing meats, you will be able to add a variety of dehydrated meats to your family's emergency, 90-day, and longer-term food storage. Dehydrated meats are a great way to supplement your family's meat storage at a fraction of the cost of freeze-dried. However, keep in mind you will need to rotate them each year, where the freeze-dried meats will store for 25 years.

HINT: Do you backpack, camp, or have a scout who does? Homemade dehydrated meals are a great way to add a variety of lightweight meals at a fraction of the cost of the pre-packaged ones.

Poultry

	FREEZE-DRIED	CANNED	DRIED	BOTTLED	TVP
CHICKEN	✓	✓	✓	✓	✓
CHICKEN, WHOLE		✓			
TURKEY	✓	✓	✓	✓	

Pork

	FREEZE-DRIED	CANNED	DRIED	BOTTLED	TVP
BACON		✓	✓		✓
HAM, DICED	✓	✓	✓	✓	✓
HAM, WHOLE		✓			
LUNCH MEAT		✓			
PORK	✓	✓		✓	
PORK CHOPS	✓				
SAUSAGE, COUNTRY	✓	✓		✓	✓
SAUSAGE, VIENNA		✓			

Beef

	FREEZE-DRIED	CANNED	DRIED	BOTTLED	TVP
BEEF, CHUNKS	✓	✓	✓	✓	✓
BEEF IN GRAVY		✓		✓	
BRISKET	✓	✓	✓	✓	✓
CORNED BEEF		✓		✓	
HAMBURGER		✓	✓		✓
MEATBALLS	✓	✓		✓	
PEPPERONI	✓		✓	✓	

Seafood

	FREEZE-DRIED	CANNED	DRIED	BOTTLED	TVP
CLAMS		✓			
CRAB	✓	✓		✓	
OYSTERS		✓		✓	
SALMON		✓		✓	
SARDINES		✓		✓	
SHRIMP		✓			
TUNA		✓		✓	

The Butcher Block

(YOUR MEAT OPTIONS)

the bakery shop

Just thinking of birthday cakes, blueberry muffins, and freshly baked bread gets us to thinking of the little bakery shop around the corner, with its wonderful smells and delectable treasures. Lucky for us, even in the world of food storage, there are lots of easy choices to fill your need for sweets and treats. If things like biscuits with honey, pancakes, brownies, and chocolate pudding are foods your family loves and eat on a regular basis, then we say go for it! You may be a family that makes these from scratch or you may use pre-packaged mixes where you just have a few ingredients. Either way, you can enjoy fresh, hot bread straight from your oven.

Let's face it, even if you do most of your cooking from scratch, there are just some days that don't allow the extra few minutes it takes to pull all the ingredients out and clean up before the company arrives. For days like these, we LOVE mixes and think you will too.

mixes

Mixes are a great addition to your food storage! Most mixes are pre-assembled, so you just pour it in a bowl, add a few more ingredients, stir, and start cooking. How much faster and easier can cooking be? Food storage companies know this, which is why so many now have added in A LOT of mixes to purchase. But do you really need those mixes in a #10 can? Are they a good deal? Is it okay to purchase mixes from the store for your food storage?

Is it possible to use your basic food storage ingredients to make some of your favorite mixes at home? These are all questions we are here to answer. If you stick with us and follow our Store This, Not That guidelines, you can have your cake and eat it too—and all with huge savings to your pocketbook!

BAKING MIX PRICES

Pancake Mix — I DOZ
canned: $2.25
store: $0.85
home: $0.50

Muffin Mix — I DOZ
canned: $4.50
store: $1.50
home: $1.50

Brownie Mix — I BOX
canned: $4.50
store: $1.30
home: $2

Cookie Mix — I DOZ
canned: $6
store: $1.30
home: $1.30

Cake Mix — I BOX
canned: $3
store: $1.30
home: $3

Frosting — I TUB
canned: $6
store: $1.60
home: $1.30

Wheat Bread Mix — I LOAF
canned: $5
store: $3
home: $1

White Bread Mix — I LOAF
canned: $4
store: $3
home: $0.60

Artisan Bread Mix — I LOAF
canned: $4
store: $4
home: $0.50

Scone Mix — I DOZ
canned: $3.80
store: $2.50
home: $0.40

Corn Muffin Mix — I DOZ
canned: $4.30
store: $1.30
home: $1.30

Biscuit Mix — I DOZ
canned: $2.50
store: $1.20
home: $1

👎 CANNED MIXES
(THE KIND FOOD STORAGE COMPANIES SELL)

Mixes in a #10 can: The secrets you "knead" to know

1 OVERPRICED

We know the list of available food storage mixes can be very enticing, especially after pages and pages of boring, bland items. Who wouldn't want to add in brownies, cookies, cake, or muffins to their food storage? We sure do! But please, don't get suckered in to those mixes sold in #10 cans. Overall, these mixes cost, on average, 3x more than what you can buy at your local grocery or big box store. YIKES!

2 TOO LITTLE

Did you know that #10 cans don't store a lot of mix? For example, there is only enough mix in that brownie can to make three batches, and then you throw the can away. What a waste! Plus, you may not even get enough mix in your can to make a whole number of batches. Whoops! Can you imagine getting to the bottom of the can with only two cups left when you need three to complete the recipe?

3 STORAGE LIFE

We know what you are thinking: "But, don't the cans help the mixes store longer—like 30 years?" The answer is yes . . . and no. You are right that they will store longer, but only about twice as long. This means the shelf life in a #10 can is only two years, not even close to the "up to 25 years" that some companies claim. In addition, mixes containing leavening, such as baking soda or powder, can and do react to any moisture in the can and to heat, causing the cans to bulge within a year of packaging.

👍 BYO MIXES
(BUY YOUR OWN MIXES)

Some mixes, when bought on sale, are even cheaper than you can make them yourself. Keep in mind that just like the #10 can varieties, some just need water added, while to others you may need to add oil or eggs. Mixes are available in bargain and expensive brands. If you already use favorite mixes, then store them, but please reconsider not using the ones on our NOT THAT list. These mixes are so easy and cheap to make yourself; you would just be, well, half-baked to buy them from the store.

👍 **STORE THIS:** brownies, cakes, cornbread, frosting (in plastic can), gelatin, pancakes, and pudding

👎 **NOT THAT:** biscuits, breads (raised), cookies, muffins, oatmeal packets, and whole-grain pancakes

HOW DO I KNOW IF MY MIX IS STILL GOOD?
It's always important to stay safe when storing food. While these mixes should be items you use and rotate on a regular basis, here are our best tips for making sure they are good.

1. CHECK THE DATE ON THE BOX
Most store-bought mixes are packaged for at least a six-month shelf life. All of them have a "best by" or "better if used by" date printed on the box. According to the USDA, "a Best if Used By (or Before) date is recommended for best flavor or quality. It is not a purchase or safety date." So unless it has an "expiration date" (which does indicate it would need to be thrown away past that date) you don't need to throw it away.

2. SMELL IT
Just like anything else, if it smells rancid or has an off smell, toss it.

3. OFF COLOR OR BLACK SPOTS
Look at the color, if it is off or has black spots (blueberries don't count), it could have mold. Surprisingly, people with allergic reactions to mold have been seriously injured eating mixes with mold in them. Plus, we can't imagine it tastes good, so play it safe and throw it away.

STOCK YOUR PANTRY
Keep it yummy and practical with these tips:

1) TRY BEFORE YOU BUY.
You won't save any money stocking up on a brand you don't like.

2) BUY WHAT YOU NEED.
Think about what you already use mixes for: birthdays, a Sunday treat, etc., and plan accordingly.

3) REPLACE WHAT YOU USE.
Mixes are too good not to use right now; plus, it helps you rotate your food storage. Just be sure to replace what you use.

4) STORE MIXES SMARTER.
To prolong the shelf life of your mixes and to keep pesky bugs out, store mixes in an airtight bucket. Remove the cardboard boxes and store only the bagged mixes to fit more in your bucket. Be sure to keep one set of instructions in or attached to the bucket.

GAMMA LID
Don't forget your gamma lid to make getting in and out of your bucket easier!

DIY MIXES
(DO-IT-YOURSELF MIXES)

Get out of the supermarket and back into your own kitchen! Mixes seem magical, like the only way you can get them is at your local supermarket. But the truth is a good mix can be found in your very own recipe box—people just don't know the secret of how to convert their favorite recipes into mixes. Making your own mixes will save money, give you more control over the ingredients (cut out partially hydrogenated fats and high fructose sugars and add in healthy ingredients like whole wheat, etc.), and save time in the kitchen.

HOW DO I KNOW WHICH RECIPE WILL MAKE A GOOD MIX?

This is very simple; any recipe that calls for mixing the dry ingredients with wet ingredients is perfect for making a mix!

1. SUBSTITUTE FOOD STORAGE ITEMS

Identify where you can use food storage to make your mix even better. Powdered milk, powdered eggs, or even powdered butter can be added to mixes for extra convenience, and whole wheat flour is a great addition to make any recipe healthier.

2. MAKE YOUR MIX

Combine all dry ingredients for one recipe and mix WELL by mixing dry ingredients together in a large electric mixer bowl or large container with lid or in a large plastic bag and shaking. Now, simply measure the amount of mixed ingredients you have and you will know how many cups you will need to make your baked good. Make sure you don't forget to figure out how much extra water you will need to add to the mix for your food storage products.

3. MAKE YOUR MIX IN BULK.

Mix together 4 times all the dry ingredients, including the dry milk and egg powders, and store in airtight container with instructions. Instructions should be to add the amount of dry ingredients you determined in step two plus the needed liquid ingredients to complete your recipe. Follow original baking instructions.

MAKING MIXES WITH FOOD STORAGE
Use your food storage in mixes with these easy tips:

1) SHORTENING OR BUTTER.

You can use dehydrated shortening, butter, or margarine powder. Substitute ½ cup powder and 2 T. water for every half cup needed. If you want to use real shortening, use your wire whisk attachment on your electric mixer to incorporate the shortening evenly. Remember that using shortening will decrease the shelf-life of your mix to a few weeks.

2) POWDERED EGGS.

To use whole egg powder in your mix, use 1–2 T. egg powder per egg. Add 2–3 T. of water per egg to liquids when mixing.

3) POWDERED MILK.

To use powdered milk in mixes, use 3 T. non-instant or 5 T. instant dry milk powder plus 1 cup of water to equal 1 cup of milk.

4) WHOLE WHEAT FLOUR.

Whole wheat flour can be substituted for white flour. Simply reduce each cup of flour needed by 1–2 T. for a better baked result. Store these mixes in the fridge or freezer to help preserve the nutritional qualities of the wheat.

Check out our mix recipes.

Need a good place to start? Get our favorite mix recipes on our website, www.storethisnotthat.com.

STOCKING THE PANTRY

Stocking your pantry with the right basic items will allow you to make any and all of your family's favorite baked goods and add a punch of flavor to your favorite meals. We're talking fats and oils, leaveners, sugars, spices, and even chocolate! (Because no food storage should be without chocolate!) But just like anything, it's essential to know the best items to store, how long they really store for, and how to know if these items are still good.

We've broken everything down for you so you can easily see the best of the best and simply forget the rest. There are also helpful hints and tips to save you money and help you do more at home. And, since so many of these items are sold by food storage companies and right at your local grocery or big box store, we've included the best places to purchase these items to save you the most money where applicable. So let's get started! We can't wait to share some of our best tips with you!

BUY AND SAVE WITH
CRISCO SHORTENING

Powdered shortening is basically a mixture of hydrogenated soybean oil and milk products. It can be used in mixes (not frying), but truthfully it's not as good as the creamy varieties, has about the same shelf life, and costs twice as much. When storing shortening, invest in Crisco. Other cheaper brands go rancid much sooner. In our experience, Crisco will store unopened in a cool, dark place for at least five years. But if you notice an off smell or taste, it may be rancid and needs to be thrown out.

STORE THIS: Crisco Shortening (regular or butter flavored)

NOT THAT: Powdered shortening or off-brand creamy varieties

EDIBLE OILS

Oils are an important part of mixes and food storage in general. Fats keep your body lubed up and running better. Lack of fats cause lower energy, dry skin, hunger, low body temperature, and mental fatigue. Oils will store 2 years or longer in cool, dark places, but still they need to be rotated frequently so they don't go rancid.

STORE THIS: **NOT THAT:**

CANOLA OR VEGETABLE OIL   CORN OIL

OLIVE OIL   GRAPE SEED OIL

COCONUT OIL   OTHER SPECIALITY OILS

BETTER BUTTER

Butter or margarine powder or butter-flavored Crisco all work in baked goods but the shortening is one third the price of the powders and gives a better texture, especially in cookies. You can also use beans as a substitute for butter or oil (see page 52). You're adding in fiber and protein and cutting the fat and cost of oil and butter!

CHEWING
THE FAT

Oils and fats are an essential for most baked goods and in other types of cooking. They give baked goods their tender, flaky texture and add flavor to cooked dishes.

There are two types of fats commonly used in baking and cooking: oils and solid fats.

Oils are fats that are liquid at room temperature, like the vegetable oils used in cooking. Oils come from many different plants and from fish.

Solid fats are fats that are solid at room temperature, like butter and shortening. Solid fats come from many animal foods and can be made from vegetable oils through a process called hydrogenation. Some common fats are butter, milk fat, beef fat (tallow, suet), chicken fat, pork fat (lard), stick margarine, shortening, and partially hydrogenated oil.

It can be difficult to know which are the best for your storage, especially since there are so many options, including powdered varieties sold by food storage companies and the regular oils and shortenings sold at your local grocery store. So we've broken down your best options. As always, it's important to keep in mind what your family already uses and is familiar with. Storing something you hate because it is cheap will only waste money in the end when you throw it out.

SWEET AS SUGAR

While it is true a spoonful of sugar helps the medicine go down, sweeteners are also one of the most important ingredients used in bakery foods. While there are many different sweeteners available, sugar is perhaps the most versatile.

WHITE SUGAR

White sugar is the cheapest of the sweeteners and has been used and loved by mankind throughout the ages. It can be used in all baked goods and if kept dry, in airtight containers, will store indefinitely, even in heat.

HINT: You may notice that if you store sugar in a #10 can that it may have an off aroma or taste. This doesn't mean it has gone rancid. It will still be safe to use. Usually, if you leave the can open or transfer the sugar the smell and taste will go away. We store sugar in large 5-gallon buckets because sugar is easily rotated and there is no tin taste.

Shelf Life: White sugar will store 30+ years in an airtight container. Be sure to not include an oxygen absorber. This will make the sugar harden.

Best Place to Purchase: Local grocery stores during holiday sales, $.50 per pound or less.

POWDERED SUGAR

Powdered sugar (also known as confectioner's sugar) is a little more expensive than white but also stores indefinitely and is great for icing and frosting.

Shelf Life: if kept dry, it will store indefinitely.

Best Place to Purchase: Local grocery stores during holiday sales.

BROWN SUGAR

Brown sugar adds a moistness and richness to baked goods. Unlike the previous sugars, even when stored in airtight containers, it will only stay soft for a few years. It will eventually become hard as a rock.

Shelf Life: if kept dry in airtight container, it will store indefinitely, but will become hard.

Best Place to Purchase: Local grocery stores during holiday sales.

MAKE YOUR OWN SUGARS

Did you know that it's possible to make your own powdered sugar and brown sugar right at home? We like the trick so much for brown sugar that we don't even store regular brown sugar anymore!

POWDERED SUGAR

Process 1 cup sugar with 1 T. cornstarch in your blender until a fine powder forms. This ends up being much cheaper than store-bought powdered sugar.

BROWN SUGAR

To make, thoroughly mix 1 cup white sugar and 1 T. molasses, or even easier, just add both ingredients when making your batter and cream all at once. That's it, instant, soft, DIY brown sugar.

MOLASSES 👍

In days gone past, molasses was the day-to-day sweetener in American homes. Molasses adds sweetness, and unlike sugar is chock full of trace minerals and vitamins.

Storage Life: indefinite

Save Money: Molasses is much cheaper if purchased by the quart or gallon from a big box store.

THE BUZZ ABOUT HONEY

Pure honey, besides being a sweetener, has healthy benefits that sugar does not. It is packed with sweetness, meaning you can use less honey than sugar in a recipe for the same sweet result. But it's important to store the RIGHT kind of honey to gain all of the benefits honey has to offer.

👍 STORE THIS

PURE HONEY

⌄⌄

Honey comes in different varieties (flavors) from the light colored and mild tasting clover to the dark, almost molasses-tasting buckwheat. The darker the color of the honey the more vitamins, minerals, and antioxidants it has. Honey is great for cooking and spreading on bread. Some companies have started watering down their honey with corn syrup, so make sure you read the label to make sure it is pure honey.

Storage life: indefinite, but may crystallize over time

Best Place to Purchase: Big box stores where you can purchase in bulk.

👎 NOT THAT

HONEY POWDER OR HONEY CRYSTALS

Honey powder or crystals cost half the price of real honey, which sounds like a great deal, doesn't it? The problem is it's not just honey; it's more like honey-flavored sugar. That's right; its number one ingredient is cane sugar, corn syrup, or refinery syrup (a fancy name for corn syrup). Food storage companies are pulling the same trick as other honey manufacturers and adding in sugar to help reduce the cost. If you want honey, stick with the real stuff.

Hint: honey stored in metal cans turns black, tastes bad, and ruins the can.

HOW TO LIQUIFY CRYSTALLIZED HONEY

Put the container in a larger container of warm water and continue until the honey is completely melted, refreshing the water as needed. Putting a clean stainless steel knife into the honey will speed up the process. It isn't recommended to microwave honey.

HOMEMADE CREAMED HONEY

You may be familiar with creamed or whipped honey; it is delicious and easy to spread. We love it on toast as a great alternative to butter (it tastes slightly like honey butter), and especially as an alternative to the popular food storage honey butter recipe that calls for a lot of sugar along with just a little honey! But did you know that this process of whipping, also known as spinning honey, prevents (under normal conditions) the honey from crystallizing? It does, which will prolong the storage life of your honey.

It is so easy to do yourself. Using a heavy-duty mixer with whip attachment, simply fill the bowl ¾ full of liquid honey and add one heaping tablespoon of commercially spun honey. Turn the mixer onto low until the spun honey is incorporated, then up one speed and continue for 10–12 minutes. Pour or scoop honey into clean jars or plastic containers with tight-fitting lids. Store spun honey in refrigerator for two weeks to allow "setting" to take place. Then eat or store at room temperature.

ADOPT A HIVE

Cox's Honey is currently making a concentrated effort to preserve the pesticide-threatened hives, bees, and honey for our future generations through its unique and innovative Beehive Adoption program. Choose a level of adoption and reap all of the rewards of having your own beehive—including a certificate of adoption and honey right to your door from your very own bees!
http://beehiveadoption.com

LEAVE IT TO LEAVENING

Leavening agents play a huge role in baking. Without them, we would be left with dense, flat, and low-volume baked goods. If you want to make your family's favorite bread, pancakes, cookies, and more, be sure to store enough baking soda, baking powder, and yeast.

BAKING SODA

It is used in baking to help with rising (usually in combination with an acid such as buttermilk, vinegar, or chocolate), in spreading and giving a beautiful golden color to baked goods.

Shelf Life: if kept dry, it will store indefinitely.

Best Place to Purchase: in bulk from big box store.

YEAST

Yeast is a living organism that stays dormant until woken up by warm water and fed with starch and/or sugar. It is a necessity for almost any type of dough or bread. It does three things.

It breaks down the starches into sugar that it then feeds on and releases gas bubbles that cause the dough to rise.

The yeast strengthens the gluten strands in the dough that holds the gas bubbles so it can hold more and more bubbles, rising higher and higher.

It adds distinctive flavors and aromas to the dough.

Shelf Life: Yeast will store 10+ years in the freezer or up to 2 years in airtight container, like a canning jar with tight-fitting lid, in the refrigerator.

Best Place to Purchase: in bulk from big box store

BAKING POWDER

This is usually a combination of baking soda, cream of tartar, and cornstarch, which provides a one-two punch for rising. The powder first gives off its rising gases when it meets the liquid as the batter is stirred and rises even more as it is heated in the oven.

Shelf Life: if kept dry in airtight container, it will store indefinitely.

Best Place to Purchase: in bulk from big box store

IS YOUR LEAVEN UP TO LIFTING?

If you have any question if your leavening is still good, there are ways to test it before you put it in your baked good. To test or proof your leavening for lifting power, do the following:

BAKING SODA

Stir ¼ T. baking soda into ½ cup water; add ¼ T. vinegar. If it bubbles up, it's good.

BAKING POWDER

Stir ¼ T. baking powder into ½ cup very hot water. If it bubbles up, it's good.

Run out of baking powder? No Problem. Simply mix thoroughly: 1 T. baking soda, 2 T. cream of tartar, and 1 T. cornstarch. Makes 4 T. baking powder.

YEAST

Stir 1 T. sugar into ¼ cup warm water (100°F); stir in 1 package yeast (2¼ T.). Let sit for 10 minutes; it should produce a bubbly foam.

MAKING BREAD

BETTER

Who doesn't love the aroma and taste of freshly baked bread? It is warm, tender, moist, and mouthwatering and the staple of meals around the world. Many people have tried their hand at mixing and kneading bread dough only to be disappointed by a loaf that is heavy, tough, and crumbly. There is a better way. Want to know the secret to making better whole-wheat bread? It's called dough enhancer. You may have heard about this but didn't know what it was or why you needed it. Let us break it down for you.

BEYOND DOUGH ENHANCER

MILK: Bread will rise higher and have a finer texture and it will keep longer. It also adds nutritional value to the finished bread.

OIL OR BUTTER: Adds tenderness and improves the elasticity of the bread. Increases bulk and helps the bread to brown more evenly. However, too much oil will make the bread crumbly. Use a maximum of 1 Tbsp. oil or shortening or butter per 1 cup of flour.

SALT: Controls the yeast process, improves flavor, and increases the shelf life of the bread. A bread made with no salt will taste flat. Do NOT add the salt to the yeast water or it will inhibit the initial yeast process. Maximum of ½ T. per 1 cup of flour.

NEVER ENDING YEAST

When you make a batch of bread dough, after the first rise, pinch off one handful of the dough and save it in an airtight container in a cool dark place, such as the refrigerator, where it will remain fresh for two or three days. The next time you make bread dough, leave out the yeast; instead, thoroughly knead the old dough into the new batch of dough. The yeast in the old dough will multiply and spread throughout the new dough. Then again after the first rise, pinch off one handful of dough and save it. Repeating this process each time you make yeast bread, a pound of yeast will last a very, very long time.

◤ EZ Wheat Bread.

Need a good bread recipe? Try our EZ Wheat Bread Recipe found in the *"Store It to Eat It"* section.

THE TRUTH
ABOUT DOUGH ENHANCER

Dough enhancer is a natural product that helps whole-grain bread to be soft, light, fluffy, and delicious. It has the added benefit of keeping your home-baked bread fresh for up to a week without preservatives. It is made from four basic ingredients (of course they call them something else, but this is what they are): wheat gluten, an acid, a starch, and sugar.

👍 STORE THIS HOMEMADE DOUGH ENHANCER
It's easy and much cheaper to use the homemade version versus what you buy at the store.

WHEAT GLUTEN

Wheat Gluten is the natural protein found in whole wheat. It helps the bread fibers strengthen, so they can hold more gas bubbles and gain an elastic texture as the dough is kneaded. It is like the latex in a balloon that when stretched before you inflate it, has less resistance, holds more air and gets bigger faster. Add 1 T. gluten to every cup of whole wheat flour. You can find vital wheat gluten at food storage companies and grocery stores. Wheat gluten stores 5 years.

VINEGAR

Acid (vinegar, lemon juice, vitamin C or ascorbic acid) strengthens the bubble so it doesn't pop too soon. Add the same amount of vinegar as you do yeast, or ¼ T. vitamin or ascorbic acid powder per loaf. We like vinegar because it is something we already use and it's cheap! Vinegar stores indefinitely.

POTATO FLAKES

Starch (potato flakes) coats the gluten so the yeast bubbles aren't popped by the sharp edges of the wheat bran, allowing the bread to rise higher. Think of it like the goop they squirt into a balloon that adds a protective layer to the latex and lets the balloon enlarge and keeps it from deflating too soon. Add 2–4 T. of potato flakes per loaf of bread. These can be found at your grocery store or food storage company. If they are stored airtight, they will store 30 years.

SUGAR

Sugar (or honey) gives the yeast a burst of energy that creates the air bubbles that fill the bread dough (or balloon). Sugar, when stored in airtight containers, stores indefinitely.

👎 NOT THAT STORE-BOUGHT DOUGH ENHANCER
Now that you can make it yourself and add it to any recipe, why pay the premium for a commercial enhancer?

BRING THE FLAVOR

Herbs, spices, and flavorings are an important part of food storage. Many of the food items that store well in long-term storage are a bit bland. Although beans, rice, and grains might be enough to sustain life, they definitely need a little something to make them taste great. Considering a lot of us have picky eaters in our hoard, making food taste great can save your ears from a lot of whining, so

STORE ALL OF THESE.

PLEASE PASS THE SALT

Too little salt—iodized salt, that is—is dangerous. It's the iodine in iodized salt that helps the body make the thyroid hormone, which is critical to an unborn child's brain development. So be sure to include iodized salt along with whichever other kind of salt you'd like to store-kosher, natural or sea.

Shelf Life: if kept dry, it will store indefinitely.

Best Place to Purchase: Grocery store or big box store.

SPICE IT UP

Whole spices can last several years. Once spices are ground, their volatile oils are released and their flavor dissipates. We recommend not buying a larger amount of an individual ground spice than you expect to use within a few years.

Old spices will not make you sick, they just won't accomplish their true purpose—flavoring your food. To determine whether or not ground spices are still viable gently shake the container with the cap on. Remove the cap after a moment and smell the container to see if the rich smell of the spice is still present.

Shelf Life: Spices will continue to add great flavor to your food for a few years if stored in a cool, dark area.

Best Place to Purchase: Grocery stores. Watch for great sales around Thanksgiving and Christmas Holidays.

VANILLA

Vanilla is needed in most delicious baked goods.

 STORE THIS: Liquid vanilla extract. It will store indefinitely and can be purchased at the store. If you really want great flavor, be sure to purchase REAL vanilla extract, not vanilla flavoring.

 NOT THAT: Vanilla powder. It costs more than vanilla extract and there are no big benefits to it.

STORING YOUR HERBS

What would pesto be without basil, or salsa sans cilantro? Whether used by the pinch or by the bunch, fresh herbs pull a recipe together by infusing the dish with unparalleled aromas and flavors. There are three basic ways to make sure you have herbs available when you need them.

BUY THEM

 STORE THIS: Dried herbs from the grocery store can be a great addition to your storage. Watch for great sales around Thanksgiving and Christmas.

NOT THAT: Freeze-dried herbs especially from a food storage company. Not only are these over-priced, they are no more flavorful than the dried variety. You have much better options for fresh tasting herbs at a fraction of the cost.

GROW YOUR OWN

Fresh-from-the-garden herbs add flavor and fragrance to foods that just can't be beat. Did you know that herbs are hardy and can be very easy to grow? Here's our list of the easiest herbs to grow:

- Basil
- Chives
- Dill
- Garlic
- Lavender
- Mint
- Oregano
- Parsley
- Rosemary
- Sage
- Thyme

THE EASY WAY TO DRY HERBS

After washing and drying fresh herbs, place on a clean paper towel and microwave on high for 30 seconds to one minute (or until completely dry—microwave times may vary depending on your microwave or the type of herb). Crumble the dried herbs and store in an airtight container for up to 3 months. Using this method will keep your herbs a vibrant green and full of flavor.

LET'S GET SAUCY!

Imagine sitting down to a meal of spaghetti without sauce, biscuits without the gravy, or chicken noodle soup without the broth. Not too appetizing, right? We use sauces and flavoring in almost every soup and main dish we make. We think you will agree that these sauces and bouillon can make or break a meal. What is the best way to include them in our 90-day and

long-term storage plans so we don't end up eating a bowl of plain pasta? What it really boils down to is this: "What kind of sauces does your family already eat?" Whether you buy sauces from the store or make them from scratch, we promise you, that when "something" has happened to turn your life upside down, having some quick and easy ways to put a hot meal on the table will not only be pleasing to the belly but help you keep your sanity.

BOUILLON

 STORE THIS:

Buying bouillon in large jars at your local grocery, big box store, or from a food storage company is the cheapest way to buy it ($.02 per teaspoon), but because bouillon loses flavor when exposed to air when it is opened again and again, we suggest buying them in smaller cans or jars ($.05 per teaspoon) or repackaging when opened. In bulk, bouillon is only offered in beef, chicken, and sometimes vegetable and ham.

Hint: For long term storage, avoid moist bouillons that have to be refrigerated when opened.

NOT THAT: Some beef and chicken gravy or bouillon products do not contain any real meat flavor. They are instead flavored with soy or vegetable

products and as you can imagine, they have don't much flavor (we like to describe the taste like dirty dish water). Some also contain MSG. So be sure to read the ingredient list before purchasing! Consider spending a little more on a higher quality product.

THE RIGHT SAUCE

 STORE THIS! Find sauces from your local store that your family tries and likes and will work in your meals. These sauces can include spaghetti, sloppy joe, alfredo, cheese, creamed soups, white sauce, and also salsa, teriyaki, or barbecue sauce. These come in cans, jars, and mixes. A great time to stock up is when they are on sale. If possible, buy in smaller (one meal size) jars for easier rotation and less waste. Of course, you can also store the products you need to make your own sauces, but having some heat and eat varieties are a great addition to your stock of easy, quick meals.

 **NOT THAT: #10 cans of sauce mixes**
- Expensive. In fact, 3x–6x more expensive than store bought mixes or jars
- Limited variety (white sauce, spaghetti, sloppy joe, cream soup)
- Unfamiliar, sometimes unpleasant, taste
- Unhealthy, high in unnatural ingredients and sometimes sugar

Reminder: Tomato powder is a great way to add flavor and nutrition to your sauces

GOOD GRAVY!

 Little packaged mixes at your grocery store. They cost about the same as the #10 cans but they are available in a much bigger variety. You can pick the quality and the flavors your family already enjoys and when stored in airtight containers, they will store as long as the large #10 cans as gravy.

Gravy in #10 cans have very limited variety (beef and chicken) and unless you are feeding an army or repackage, it will go stale before you reach the bottom of the can.

THE CHOICES
FOR CHOCOHOLICS

Many of us crave chocolate, especially when stressed; so being able to make brownies, chocolate cake, or chocolate chip cookies is more a necessity than a luxury, right? We agree, and lucky for us, there are a couple of ways to do this with cocoa powders and chocolate chips.

HOW TO STORE
CHOCOLATE CHIPS AND OTHER CHOCOLATE

Chocolate Chips, kisses and plain chocolate bars will store 1–2 years on your shelf or freezer. Repackaging your chocolate in airtight jars or bags and storing in dark places can keep them looking and tasting fresh for several more years.

1   Put chocolate into a canning jar. You can use a canning funnel to make it even easier.

2   Top with a regular canning lid (not the ring).

3   Use a Foodsaver or Seal-a-meal machine with a hose and a jar attachment to suck the air out.

CHOCOLATE HAZELNUT SPREADS

Chocolate hazelnut spreads are another great way to get your chocolate fix. It has a shorter shelf life, about 12 months, but is easily rotated as you use it on pancakes, bread, cinnamon rolls, or by the spoonful (hey, we're just being honest here).

COCOA POWDERS

There are two distinct kinds of cocoa powders available, NATURAL and DUTCH PROCESSED.

Natural cocoa powder is milder in flavor and lighter in color. It is high in acid and is best used in batter recipes that use baking soda or in ice cream or chocolate sauces.

Dutch processed cocoa powder is dark brown and has a richer, deeper chocolate flavor. During processing its acid is neutralized, making it a better choice when using recipes that use baking powder.

Storage Life: For both cocoa powders, if kept airtight, in cool, dark place is two years. You know the drill: if it smells rancid throw it out; otherwise it is safe to use.

Best Place to Purchase: big box store in bulk

FREEZE-DRIED ICE CREAM

When you're craving some chocolate ice cream—will freeze-dried ice cream hit the spot? No, not if your vision of ice cream is soft, creamy, and cold. Freeze-dried ice cream and ice cream sandwiches kind of look like the real thing but they are hard, crunchy, and definitely not cold. They taste like ice cream but have the texture of meringue and at 6x the cost of real ice cream. Why not just eat a cookie or make some real ice cream instead? Look in the Store It To Eat It section for our recipe.

DRINK IT UP

Have you ever considered storing juice or flavored fruit mixes as part of your food storage? Drinks, like juices and fruit flavored drinks, can act as a comfort food—especially to young children, break up the monotony of stale water, and, in some cases, add vitamins that prevent scurvy to your diet.

BOTTLED JUICES

It's important to understand the difference between juice and fruit flavored drinks so you can make the best choice for your family.

The term fruit "juice" is a broad term that can mean anything from 100% fruit content to less than 1% fruit content with a lot of added sugar that greatly increases the shelf life. Thus the shelf life of fruit juice depends on a variety of factors such as the best by date, how the juice was stored, the packaging and the content of the juice package. Most juices are high in vitamins, mainly vitamin C, and can substitute as a serving of fruit. Juices which are all fruit will spoil sooner than juices with added sugar and preservatives as the natural sugars in the fruit will begin to ferment over time. Just beware of added sugar in your juice.

Shelf Life: Read ingredients carefully and observe the best by date.

FRUIT DRINKS

Fruit-flavored drinks (the powdered drinks sold by food storage companies) are NOT powdered juices but instead fruit-flavored drinks. These fruit-flavored drinks aren't different from what you can purchase in the store, they are just packaged in #10 cans. In fact, you may find a greater variety at the grocery store such as Tang, powdered lemonade or ready-made sugar-free mixes, such as Crystal Light, and the many flavors of Kool-Aid. The question is, what will work best for your family? Aside from taste, here are some things to consider.

- Kool-Aid, unsweetened: is cheapest (price includes cost with sugar), small package, concentrated flavor, big variety, can be used to make electrolyte drink, stores for many years in airtight container.
- Ready-made mixes with sugar: cost 2x more than Kool-Aid; likable, familiar flavors; easy to mix; several flavors; stores for years in airtight containers.
- #10 cans, sugar included: costs 4x more than Kool-Aid; variety of flavors; mixed reviews in taste tests; stores for years.
- Juice bottles or cans: expensive, bulky, heavy, have shortest shelf life.

DRINK OPTIONS

	#10 Cans	Ready-made	Kool-Aid unsweetened	Bottled
Apple	X		X	X
Cherry		X	XX	
Fruit Punch	X		X	X
Grape	X		X	X
Lemon-Lime		X	X	
Lemonade	X		XX	X
Orange		X	X	X
Peach Mango	X		X	
Strawberry			X	
Average cost for 1 cup	$0.20	$0.09	$0.05	$0.22

👍 STORE THIS: GATORADE

Gatorade and other powdered energy drinks with electrolytes can be very handy after an upset stomach. Along with an upset stomach, your body may also experience diarrhea, which may result in dehydration as well as an electrolyte imbalance. Electrolytes help your heart beat as well as help muscles, cells and other organs function, so replenishing lost electrolytes is important. While water helps replenish lost fluids, sports drinks replenish lost electrolytes and other minerals.

food storage
BUCKETS
& bundles

FAST FOOD—FOOD STORAGE

Chances are you've seen those miracle buckets of food storage, the "one and done" of the food storage world. They claim to have just what you need for great tasting, easy to prepare meals that your family will love. Just hand over your money, take their products home with you and store them in a cool, dark place and you're done. But, could it really be that simple? It could be that simple, if you have a lot of space, a lot of extra water stored (to rehydrate all of those meals), and a LOT of money. We think of these buckets like eating out because, truth be told, you could be spending as much or more on one of these food storage meals as you would spend taking your family to a fancy restaurant!

Don't believe us? Meet Johnny (names have been changed to protect the innocent). Johnny decided to buy a year supply of food for his family. He was very busy and found a reputable company that sold deluxe kits with lots of good-sounding meals, that even included desserts, and plunked down $10,000. (NO JOKE!) It was expensive, but he wanted only the best for his family. When it arrived, he decided to try a meal from his stash. He quickly realized that the "meal" was only enough food for a very small child, and that to fill him up; he would need 4 times the allotted serving. His $10,000 "year supply" was, in reality, a three-month supply.

See what we mean? Expensive! Now, we're not saying there isn't a place for these buckets in your food storage, but your year-supply shouldn't be made up of them. After all, you'd never eat out every meal, so why do it with your food storage? These buckets do serve a purpose as emergency food in case you're sheltering at home, or mixed into your year supply to give yourself a break from cooking. To get the most for your money with this type of food storage, be sure to follow our rules.

YEAR SUPPLY BY NUMBERS

- 3 meals per day x 365 days = 1095 meals (not to be confused with servings)
- Minimum daily calories: 2000 calories
- 2000 calories per day x 365 days = 730,000 calories (minimum)
- Minimum meal sizes: breakfast: 1 cup; lunch and dinner: 1 ½–2 cups; sides: ¼–½ cup
- #10 cans of freeze-dried foods contain 10 1-cup servings
- 1 #10 can will feed five people for lunch or dinner (2 cups each)

TWO MAIN TYPES OF BUNDLES

There are two main types of bundles on the market. You have to decide which fits into your budget and storage space. Both types store 10–25 years if kept cool, under 75 degrees.

JUST ADD WATER, FREEZE-DRIED, AND/OR DEHYDRATED MEALS are fast and easy to use, have less fiber, are less filling and are much more expensive.

MOSTLY BASIC FOODS such as: grains, beans/lentils, fruits, vegetables, sugar, and meat products, with a few meals or soups thrown in. This contains a foundation for meals (assuming you like everything in it, these kits can be filled with things like lentils that your family isn't used to eating). But you will want to add, seasonings, sauces, etc. to make real meals. These are usually much cheaper and higher in calories and they take up less space. However, they do require cooking skills.

THE 7 RULES
for buying food storage buckets & bundles

RULE NO. 1 Serving sizes are not created equal

Meal serving sizes range from ¼ cup to 3 cups depending on the product. Many companies list their serving sizes as grams vs. cups, not helpful when determining actual eating amounts. As a general rule: the higher the number of servings in a bundle, the smaller the average size of the servings.

Beware: *up to 30% of bundle's servings can come from minute servings of seasonings and drinks.*

RULE NO. 2 One serving does not equal a meal

We tend to think a meal as a serving—wrong. Case in point: a 5-gallon bucket of emergency food said it contained 308 servings, and it did: ¼ cup of this and a tablespoon of that. You have to put a lot of these "servings" together to make a meal.

Beware: *claiming a large number of servings is a marketing trick.*

Buying a whole year supply is a big and important investment. Most food storage companies have sample packs you can buy. PLEASE try before you buy and then only buy what you like. This may mean buying foods from several different companies and putting together your own bundle.

RULE NO. 3 Quality of food ingredients

Read the labels. Do they contain lots of sugars and preservatives? Do they use real milk (instant or non-instant) or milk drinks (see milk section for details)? Sugar vs. honey/sugar powder? TVP or meat flavorings vs. real meat? Are the meals filling or watery soups? On the plus side, some packages have gluten-free and vegetarian options.

RULE NO. 4 Variety of Food

Look for packages with a variety of food options, the more the better. The better bundles have five or more breakfasts, 12 or more main meals and a variety of fruits and vegetables too. One only had two breakfasts and seven main meals and crackers and peanut butter. We would get tired of that really quick.

RULE NO. 5 Storage Life

Many of these food bundles claim to "store up to 25 years." The key term being "up to." These packages usually contain mixed types of foods. Generally they store as follows:

FREEZE-DRIED: 25 years, DEHYDRATED: 8–10 years, **MIXES**: 1–2 years

RULE NO. 6 Total Calories

The best way to determine if a food storage unit has enough life sustaining calories is to take the total calories for the bundle (usually found on website; otherwise, call them) and divide it by the number of days the bundle is supposed to feed you. This number should be at least 2,000 (the per day amount). In addition, the cheaper companies often include small sugary drink servings to boost their number of servings and calories. With some companies, 20–50 percent of their overall calories are from drink mix.

RULE NO. 7 Packing & Preserving

Emergency and long-term storage food should be packaged in one of two ways: #10 cans (double lined) or Mylar pouches in buckets (to keep the food inside protected from bugs, rodents, punctures, and smashing). Whether in cans or pouches, long term packaging should also include an oxygen absorber (nitrogen-packed food is not as effective). Oxygen absorbers are not needed in sugar or sugar fruit drinks.

For best results, store in between 50 and 70 degrees to extend storage life.

HOW MUCH WILL YOUR PET NEED?

Use our handy dandy pet chart to help you estimate* how much water and dry food your pet will need and the average cost for dry food per month. Included are the cost comparisons of regular dry pet food in a bag and freeze-dried pet food in a #10 can. These amounts are for one month.

CAT OR TINY DOG

(under 10 pounds)

Water: 3 gallons
Dry Food: 8 pounds
Cost Dry Food: $8
Freeze-Dried: 3 cans
Cost Freeze-Dried: $75

SMALL DOG

(10–25 pounds)

Water: 6 gallons
Dry Food: 15 pounds
Cost Dry Food: $15
Freeze-Dried: 7 cans
Cost Freeze-Dried: $175

MEDIUM DOG

(25–50 pounds)

Water: 12 gallons
Dry Food: 30 pounds
Cost Dry Food: $30
Freeze-Dried: 15 cans
Cost Freeze-Dried: $375

LARGE DOG

(50–75 pounds)

Water: 18 gallons
Dry Food: 45 pounds
Cost Dry Food: $45
Freeze-Dried: 22 cans
Cost Freeze-Dried: $525

X-LARGE DOG

(over 75 pounds)

Water: 28 gallons
Dry Food: 60 pounds
Cost Dry Food: $60
Freeze-Dried: 33 cans
Cost Freeze-Dried: $800

costs and amounts needed will vary depending on what and how much your pet eats.

FURRY FRIENDS

Your furry friends depend on you for their survival every day, so when planning for emergencies keep them in mind. How much water and food for your dogs and cats do you need to store? Well, on average, for every ten pounds they weigh, you will need ten ounces of water and one cup of dry food. Plan to have enough for 3–12 months, just like you: no food, no life.

👍 STORE THIS
STORE-BOUGHT PET FOOD

The easiest and cheapest way to have enough food for them is just buy more of what they already eat and rotate it. (That way you know their tummies will be used to it and you won't get any digestion surprises.) Dry foods will store about a year before getting stale and sometimes even rancid. Canned food will store for several years when kept cool. Keeping the dry food in buckets or other container with a tight fitting lid will protect it from rodents and extend its storage life.

👎 NOT THAT
FREEZE-DRIED PET FOOD

Some food storage companies have started selling freeze-dried pet food. These nuggets are made from real beef, vegetables and fruits and comes in lightweight packaging. Even though the reviews for the freeze-dried pet food in a #10 can were amazing, it's important to remember two things: it is freeze-dried, so it needs water to make it safe for your pets to eat, and at $24 per can, it is very expensive. How expensive? More than 10x the cost of store bought pet food.

PROTECTING YOUR PET

Something else to consider in caring for your pets during and after a disaster is sheltering them. If you have to evacuate, do you have a friend who would be willing to take them in case pets are not allowed in shelters? If you are staying home, are your fences intact to keep your dogs from roaming the neighborhood and joining a dog pack? If not, do you have a way to secure them? If you have bigger animals, do you have a safe place to take them and a way to transport them? Consider your options now for protecting your pets later.

« STORAGE » solutions

ORGANIZE YOUR PANTRY

Make more room in your pantry with a can rotating system. These systems make it easy to rotate your cans (first in, first out) and allow you to fit more cans on a shelf.

Can Organizer
Made from cardboard, these lightweight solutions come sized for specific cans and can be ordered in different sizes.

Available at www. canorganizer.com

Cansolidator
Also made from plastic, these are customizable, can be attached to other units and comes in different sizes.

Available at thrivelife.com, Amazon.com, and Costco.com.

Storage Tip: *If you have extra space in between the tops of these can rotators and the shelf in your pantry, store small boxed items like cereal there.*

Food Rotation Systems

These come in many different sizes sure to fit in a closet or cold storage room (Crystal fit two of them in her under-stair storage!). They are completely customizable and can fit cans as small as a tuna can to as large as a #10 can.

Storage Tip: Not all of your cans need to fit on the shelves; place a piece of sturdy wood on the top and store extra cans there to refill as needed.

Available at thrivelife.com, Amazon.com, Costco.com, and SamsClub.com (the best deal is at Costco).

HIDDEN STORAGE SPACES

Chances are you have more space for food storage in your home than you realize! Check out these hidden storage spaces in your house.

CLOSETS
Most closets have wasted space at the top where people can't reach. Make use of the space by adding in extra shelves and storing #10 cans there.

BEDS
Store extra food storage under the bed. Check out Thrive Life's under bed can rotators or use storage boxes sized to fit under the bed for easy pull-out abilities.

COUCHES
Place a short bookshelf or faux sofa table behind your couch! Fit cans on the shelves behind the couch and place decorative items on top where people can see. Or, if your couch is tall enough, place food under your couch.

Jar Box

Jar boxes are a great way to keep your canning jars, clean, organized and safe from breaking—even from the shaking of an earthquake. Each box includes two sturdy, plastic molded trays that snap together securely to hold a dozen canning jars. These boxes can then be stacked together with other jar boxes; which helps to ensure the stability and safety of the jars' contents.

The shells can also be separated into 2 trays. The quart-sized box measures 20" x 14 ¼" x 3 ¼" and the pint box is 18¼" x 13" x 2¼". They both hold regular and wide-mouth canning jars and are dishwasher safe. What a great way to protect your food canning investment!

Available for purchase at Amazon.com

STORE IT TO EAT IT

RECIPES & MENUS

Cooking with Food Storage

From cans and buckets to delicious meals.

Learn how to make dishes your family will actually eat.

Because we want you to think of your food storage more as meals rather than as cans and buckets of wheat, beans and milk. We need to teach you how to put together a great long-term supply in terms of meals the way your family would eat them. What we, and hopefully you, care about is making a great long-term plan that is successful, easy to use, and that won't break the budget. We've designed all of the recipes to be made as cheaply as possible and to include all the best food storage products for the job.

Really, we can teach you everything you need to know by showing you how to use the basics along with freeze-dried, dehydrated, or canned products in your family's favorite meals. While you may not choose to use every one of these meals for your food storage, they will show you a pattern of how you can build some of your own out of your family favorites. Or if you really want you can . . .

Make Over Your Own Recipes

Look for easy meals like spaghetti or fettuccine alfredo that your family already eats. Noodles with a bottled sauce make for very easy shelf-stable meals. Also, look for recipes where the only fresh ingredients are meat and/or vegetables. A lot of these may be soup recipes but definitely aren't limited to soup. Recipes that are saucy with meat and served over a carb are also very easy to transition to shelf-stable. Frozen or fresh vegetables can be replaced with canned and fresh meat can be exchanged with canned meat. We suggest you take a walk down your local canned food aisle. You will probably be surprised at all the things that are canned that can be used in your everyday recipes.

Make a Menu

We want you to plan your meals into menus. It helps you know how much you need to store, cuts down on waste, and gives you a plan to follow. We've broken the entire recipe section into a menu to show you an example of how to do it. Below are your goals:

BREAKFASTS	LUNCHES	DINNERS	DESSERTS
Goal: Choose at least two weeks of breakfast meals.	**Goal: Choose at least two weeks of lunches.**	**Goal: Choose at least four weeks (28) of dinners.**	**Goal: Choose at least four to have every month.**
For your long-term plan, we want you to plan for at least two weeks of breakfast meals that you can rotate for the year. We won't judge you for choosing cold cereal for the two weeks, if you don't. The most important thing is to be REAL with yourself and what your family normally eats.	It may be hard to think of a variety of lunches to serve, but we think the key to variety is in the snacks. Basic lunches start with a sandwich and are coupled with snacks like chips, crackers, fruit, and yogurt. You may be surprised at how many options you will have to put in that brown paper sack.	We've taken all of the dinner time classics and revamped them. We've got family comfort classics, budget friendly beans and rice (really, they can taste good!), and the meals your kids love. They are separated into themes to make it easy for you to plan for variety.	After all, the family that eats dessert together stays together. Plan for a few treats every once in a while—it will keep you all from going crazy. Plan on having one dessert a week. You'll want to pick easy-to-make desserts that are real comfort treats for your family.

Breakfast
WEEK ONE

SUNDAY

2

MONDAY

3

TUESDAY

Whether you're looking for easy, cheap, or simply delicious, we've got you covered. Our two week menu for breakfasts is sure to please even the pickiest eaters and give you some great ideas on how delicious food storage really can be!

LEARN HOW TO MAKE DRINKABLE POWDERED MILK ON PAGE 109

4

WEDNESDAY

5

THURSDAY

6

FRIDAY

7

SATURDAY

1. Country Apple Fritter Bread – pg. 102
A yummy pull-apart bread with dreamy icing and filled with dehydrated apples.

2. Instant Oatmeal Packets – pg. 102
Save big money by making your own instant oatmeal packets!

3. Whole Wheat Pancakes – pg. 102
Much better than any whole grain pancake mix on the market.

4. Granola – pg. 103
A delicious and easy cereal. It can be served warm or cold.

5. Blueberry Muffins – pg. 104
An easy-to-make morning treat.

6. Peanut Butter Chocolate Smoothie – pg. 104
Perfect for those busy mornings when you're out of milk.

7. Sausage and Biscuits – pg. 104
A nostalgic favorite remixed with food storage.

FOLLOW THE PIG! Look for this icon to find delicious, budget-friendly meals your family will love.

1. *Country Apple Fritter Bread*

PREP 15 MIN BAKE 50–60 MIN

⅓ cup light brown sugar (or ⅓ cup white sugar with ½ Tbsp. molasses)

1 tsp. ground cinnamon

⅔ cup white sugar

½ cup butter, softened (or ½ cup drained, cooked white beans)

2 eggs (2 Tbsp. dry egg powder + ¼ cup water)

1½ tsp. vanilla extract

1½ cups all-purpose flour (or ¾ cup white flour + ¾ cup whole-wheat flour)

1¾ tsp. baking powder

½ cup milk (1½ Tbsp. dry milk powder + ½ cup water)

2 apples, peeled and chopped (or 2½ cups dehydrated apples chopped and hydrated), mixed with 2 Tbsp. granulated sugar and 1 tsp. cinnamon

Old-Fashioned Creme Glaze

½ cup of powdered sugar

1–3 Tbsp. of milk or cream (depending on thickness of glaze wanted)

Instructions

1. Preheat oven to 350 degrees. Use a 9×5-inch loaf pan and spray with non-stick spray or line with foil and spray with non-stick spray to get out easily for slicing.

2. Mix brown sugar and cinnamon together in a bowl. Set aside.

3. In another medium-sized bowl, beat white sugar and butter (or beans) together using an electric mixer until smooth and creamy.

4. Beat in eggs, 1 at a time, until blended in (or add in egg powder and water); add in vanilla extract.

5. Add flour and baking powder to creamed butter mixture and stir until blended.

6. Mix milk into batter until smooth.

7. Pour half the batter into the prepared loaf pan; add half the apples and half the brown sugar-cinnamon mixture.

8. Lightly pat apple mixture into batter.

9. Pour the remaining batter over apple layer and top with remaining apples and brown sugar/cinnamon mixture.

10. Lightly pat apples into batter; swirl brown sugar mixture through apples using knife or spoon.

11. Bake in the preheated oven until a toothpick inserted in the center of the loaf comes out clean, approximately 50–60 minutes.

12. To make glaze, mix powdered sugar and milk or cream together until well mixed.

13. Let cool for about 15 minutes before drizzling with glaze.

Baking options: Bake 30–40 minutes for 2 loaf recipe, 15–20 minutes for muffins or 50–60 minutes for one full loaf recipe or until toothpick inserted in center comes out clean.

2. INSTANT OATMEAL PACKETS

PREP 5 MIN COOK 1–2 MIN

4 cups instant oatmeal

2 Tbsp. dry milk powder

2 Tbsp. sugar (You can decrease this according to your family's tastes)

Mix dry ingredients together in an empty #10 can and store covered in a cool, dry place. Or store ½-cup servings in baggies with dehydrated apples, raisins, craisins or other fruit and spices your family enjoys.

Making Oatmeal From Your Mix

½ cup oatmeal mix

1 cup water

Mix oatmeal mix and raisins (or other dehydrated fruit) with water and microwave for 2 minutes. If you need to make more of this for a larger family, simply boil the water first in a pot on the stove and then stir in the oats and let sit for 1 minute.

3. WHOLE WHEAT PANCAKES

PREP 15 MIN COOK 50–60 MIN

1½ cups milk (heaping ¼ cup dry milk powder)

1 cup whole wheat berries

2 Tbsp. oil

2 eggs (2 Tbsp. dry egg powder + ¼ cup water)

2 Tbsp. sugar

1 Tbsp. baking powder

¼ tsp. salt

Instructions

1. Add milk (or water) and wheat berries to blender. Blend on high for 1–2 minutes.

2. Add remaining ingredients (including dry milk powder) to jar and secure lid. Press "Pulse" 5–7 times to incorporate remaining ingredients.

3. Allow batter to rest 5 minutes.

4. Pour ½ cup batter onto greased, heated griddle, and cook approximately 1 minute or until bubbles break surface of pancake and underside is golden brown. Flip and cook for approximately 30 seconds. Repeat with remaining batter.

4. The Granola Formula

We love homemade granola for a lot of reasons (1. it's yummy 2. it's super easy 3. it's (usually) cheaper 4. baking it fills your home with luscious smells 5. it requires five tools and you have them all). The bottom line is that all granolas are variations on the same formula. So feel free to mix, match, adjust, and tweak until it speaks straight to your soul.

ESSENTIAL INGREDIENTS:

 +  +  + +

GRAINS (3 CUPS)
Old-fashioned or plain rolled oats.

NUTS (I CUP)
If you use raw, add before baking. If you are using roasted, add them after baking

SWEETENER (¾ CUP)
Honey, agave, maple syrup— it all works. Add a little brown sugar to the syrup for even more flavor.

OIL (¼–½ CUP)
Oil creates a crispy-crunchy texture and keeps it from turning into a sticky mess.

SALT (¾ TSP)
Salt brings out the flavors and makes your granola compulsively munchable.

OPTIONAL INGREDIENTS:

 +  +  +  =

COCONUT (I CUP)
If you have it, it will really add new dimensions.

DRIED FRUIT (I CUP)
Do not add fruit until AFTER baking or it will make them awkwardly crunchy.

SPICES (I TSP.)
For sure, cinnamon is an obvious but don't be afraid to add a pinch of others.

COCOA (¼ CUP)
Add the cocoa in with the other dry ingredients before baking.

AWESOME GRANOLA

HOW TO MIX & BAKE

1. Measure grain, nuts, seeds, salt, and spices into a large bowl.
2. Add sweeteners and oil.
3. Stir, stir, stir.
4. Spread out on a large baking sheet.
5. Bake at 300 degrees for 30–45 minutes, giving it a stir after about 20 minutes. Keep in mind that it won't be crunchy even when it's done baking; the granola will set and harden as it cools.
6. Stop when the granola looks toasty brown and smells incredible.
7. Let the granola cool completely in the pan, then store in an airtight container.

Easy Peanut Butter Granola

PREP 5 MIN BAKE 35 MIN

1½ cups white sugar
1 cup oil
½ tsp. vanilla extract
⅔ cup peanut butter
½ tsp. salt
1 cup water
12 cups rolled oats
1 tsp. cinnamon

Instructions

1. Mix sugar, oil, vanilla, peanut butter, salt and water and heat in 4-cup glass jug for 4 minutes on high.
2. Meanwhile, mix oats and cinnamon in large bowl.
3. Pour wet ingredients over dry and mix quickly and well.
4. Put on to two small greased cookie sheets.
5. Bake at 325 degrees for 25 minutes.
6. Exchange cookie sheets in oven, cook 10 minutes.
7. Turn oven off and let granola dry for several hours.
8. Store in closed jar on kitchen counter and watch it disappear.

5. BLUEBERRY MUFFINS

PREP 15 MIN BAKE 20 MIN

1½ cups all-purpose flour

¾ cup white sugar

½ tsp. salt

2 tsp. baking powder

⅓ cup vegetable oil or white bean purée

1 egg (1 Tbsp. dry egg powder + 2 Tbsp. water)

⅓ cup milk (1 Tbsp. dry milk powder + ⅓ cup water)

1 cup fresh blueberries or 1 cup freeze-dried blueberries

Instructions

1. Preheat oven to 400 degrees. Grease muffin cups or line with muffin liners.

2. Combine flour, sugar, salt and baking powder. Combine vegetable oil, egg and milk. Mix this with flour mixture. Fold in blueberries (if you're using freeze-dried blueberries, DO NOT hydrate first, simply fold in berries and allow to hydrate for a few minutes in the batter).

3. Fill muffin cups right to the top (regular size tins make 12, giant tins make 5–6 muffins).

4. Bake regular size tins for 18 minutes, giant tins for 20–25 minutes.

6. PEANUT BUTTER CHOCOLATE SMOOTHIE

PREP 15 MIN

½ cup water

¾ cup dry milk powder

⅓ cup chocolate drink mix powder

1 banana (¼ cup freeze-dried banana slices, hydrated)

2 spoonfuls of peanut butter

2 cups ice

Instructions

Layer ingredients in your blender as listed and blend until smooth. Serve immediately!

MAKE YOUR OWN CHOCOLATE DRINK MIX

⅔ cup sugar

⅓ cup cocoa

Pinch of salt

Mix together and store in an airtight container. To use, add 1–2 Tbsp. of mix to milk and stir with a wire whisk.

7. Sausage and Biscuits

PREP 15 MIN COOK 12 MIN

Sausage Gravy

1 pkg. McCormick® Country Gravy Mix

1 cup cold water

1 cup milk (3 Tbsp. dry milk powder + 1 cup water)

¾ cup sausage, crumbled and cooked or freeze-dried

Stove Top Instructions

1. Stir water gradually into Gravy Mix with whisk in medium saucepan. If you're using powdered milk, mix the dry milk powder with the dry sauce before adding all of the necessary water. If you're using freeze-dried sausage crumbles, add directly to sauce before hydrating. If the sauce is too thick, you can add in 1 Tbsp. of water at a time until the desired consistency.

2. Stirring frequently, cook on medium heat until gravy comes to boil. Reduce heat and simmer 1 minute. (Gravy will thicken upon standing.) Serve over biscuits, chicken fried steak, fried chicken or home fries.

Microwave Directions: Stir water into Gravy Mix (and dry milk powder, if using powdered milk) and sausage in 2-quart microwavable bowl. Microwave on HIGH 4 to 6 minutes or until thickened, stirring after each minute. Microwave ovens vary; cook time is approximate.

Easy Drop Biscuits

We realize drop biscuits aren't the traditional biscuit for this recipe, but they are so easy and cut the time and mess for this recipe in half!

2 cups all-purpose flour

1 Tbsp. baking powder

2 tsp. sugar

¼ tsp. salt

⅓ cup oil

1 cup milk (3 Tbsp. dry milk powder + 1 cup water)

Instructions

1. Preheat oven to 450 degrees.

2. In a large bowl, combine flour, baking powder, and sugar.

3. Stir in oil and milk just until moistened. Drop batter on a lightly greased cookie sheet by the tablespoon.

4. Bake in preheated oven until golden on the edges, about 8 to 12 minutes. Serve warm with sausage gravy poured on top.

8. *Raspberry Sweet Rolls*

PREP 30 MIN BAKE 15–20 MIN

Dough

1 cup warm milk (3 Tbsp. dry milk powder + 1 cup water)

2 eggs (2 Tbsp. dry egg powder; no water, as it makes the dough too sticky)

¼ cup oil

4½ cups flour

1 tsp. salt

½ cup sugar

2½ tsp. yeast

Filling

¾ cup raspberry jam

Icing Glaze

½ cup of powdered sugar

1 3 Tbsp. of milk

1 tsp. vanilla

Instructions

1. Pour yeast into warm milk (or warm water if you're using powdered milk). Add sugar, oil and eggs to yeast-liquid mixture. Add remaining dry ingredients (adding dry milk powder last).

2. Knead until smooth and elastic (about 7 minutes).

3. Allow dough to rest for 15 minutes.

4. Roll dough into a 16×21-inch rectangle. Spread dough with ¾ cup raspberry jam.

5. Roll up dough and cut into 12 rolls. Place rolls in a lightly greased 9×13 inch baking pan. Cover and let rise until nearly doubled, about 30 minutes.

6. Meanwhile, preheat oven to 375 degrees.

7. Bake rolls in preheated oven until golden brown, about 15–20 minutes.

8. While rolls are baking, combine together powdered sugar, milk and vanilla.

9. Spread icing on warm rolls before serving.

9. FARINA HOT CEREAL

PREP 2 MIN COOK 5 MIN

1 Serving: 1¼ cups water or milk (heaping 3 Tbsp. dry milk powder + 1¼ cups water); ⅛ tsp. salt (optional); 3 Tbsp. farina cereal.

2 Servings: 2 cups water or milk (⅓ cup dry milk powder + 2 cups water); ¼ tsp. salt (optional); ⅓ cup farina cereal.

4 Servings: 4 cups water or milk (⅔ cup dry milk powder + 4 cups water); ½ tsp. salt (optional); ¾ cup farina cereal.

Stovetop:

1. Bring water and salt to a boil. (Or, if using milk, just bring to a boil.)

2. Gradually add farina cereal, stirring constantly with wire whisk until well blended.

3. Return to a boil. Reduce heat to low; simmer uncovered 2½ minutes or until thickened, stirring frequently. Cool slightly.

Microwave:

1. Mix 3 Tbsp farina cereal, ¾ cup water or milk and a dash of salt in 1-quart microwaveable bowl or measuring cup.

2. Microwave on high 1 minute. Stir with wire whisk. Cook an additional 1 to 2 minutes or until thickened, stirring every 30 seconds. Stir again. Cool slightly. *Caution:* Bowl will be hot; carefully remove from microwave using pot holders.

3. **Note:** Microwave ovens vary. Cooking times are approximate. Overheating can cause cereal to boil over.

Tips for Best Results: When preparing with milk, watch carefully, stirring to prevent milk from boiling over. For thinner cereal stir in 1 to 2 Tbsp. additional hot water or milk for each serving. For thicker cereal, let stand a few minutes.

Stir-in ideas! Maple syrup; fruit spreads or jams; freeze-dried fruit, such as strawberries, raspberries, blueberries, or bananas.

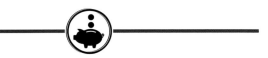

10. BUTTERMILK WAFFLES

PREP 15 MIN COOK 10 MIN

1¾ cups all-purpose flour

1 tsp. baking powder

1 tsp. baking soda

½ tsp. salt

2 eggs (2 Tbsp. dry egg powder + ¼ cup water)

2 cups buttermilk (⅓ cup dry milk powder + 2 cups water + 2 Tbsp. vinegar, let stand for five minutes)

⅓ cup canola oil or bean purée

Instructions

1. In a large bowl, combine the flour, baking powder, baking soda and salt. In another bowl, beat the eggs; add buttermilk and oil. Stir into dry ingredients just until combined.

2. Bake in a preheated waffle iron according to manufacturer's directions until golden brown. Serve with syrup and whipped cream if desired.

Yield: 16 waffles (4 inches).

Breakfast
WEEK TWO

9

MONDAY

10

TUESDAY

LEARN HOW TO MAKE HOMEMADE MAPLE SYRUP ON PAGE 109

FREEZE-DRIED FRUIT MAKES A GREAT ADDITION TO ANY BREAKFAST CEREAL!

11

WEDNESDAY

12

THURSDAY

13

FRIDAY

14

SATURDAY

8. Raspberry Sweet Rolls – pg. 105
Mouth-watering sweet rolls with everyone's favorite filling—raspberry jam.

9. Farina Hot Cereal – pg. 105
Warm up on a cold day with this cereal.

10. Buttermilk Waffles – pg. 105
Light and crisp waffles that are sure to please any crowd.

11. Easy Yogurt Parfait – pg. 108
Learn how to use your powdered milk to make thick, creamy greek yogurt for a fraction of the price.

12. Hashbrown Muffins – pg. 109
A great on-the-go hearty breakfast filled with protein and food storage.

13. Peach Smoothie – pg. 109
Deliciously sweet and filled with nutrition.

14. Baked Omelet Roll – pg. 109
Impress your toughest critics with this easy and impressive omelet.

Homemade Yogurt

We love homemade yogurt. It costs a fraction of the price of store-bought yogurt, is much healthier (far less sugar), and is a great way to use powdered milk. You will be amazed at how easy AND delicious it is. Be sure you are using REAL powdered milk. A milk alternative will fail when making yogurt.

ESSENTIAL INGREDIENTS:

- 2 quarts pasteurized milk (cream, whole, low fat, or skim)—for food storage purposes, we'll use powdered milk. For non-instant milk you'll need 1½ cups dry milk powder and 2 quarts water. If you're using instant milk you'll need 3 cups dry milk powder and 2 quarts water.

- Additional nonfat dry milk powder (for extra milk proteins)—Use 1⅓ cups powder when using non instant powdered milk, or use 2⅔ cups powder when using instant powdered milk. The higher the milk solids the firmer the yogurt will be.

- Store bought, unflavored yogurt—Use ½ cup. Be sure the product label says live cultures and includes *L.bulgaricus* and *S.thermophilus*. Some yogurts may also include *acidophilus* or *B.bifidum*, and this is perfectly fine; it will still make a successful yogurt. We prefer to use Mountain High Yoghurt as our starter.

- (Optional) 2 to 4 tablespoons sugar or honey.

STEPS FOR MAKING YOGURT:

Mix your powdered milk (all of it, both to make the initial 2 quarts of milk and the additional milk).

In a 4–5 qt. slow cooker, place milk and sugar or honey, if desired, cover and cook on low for 2.5 hours.

After the 2.5 hours, unplug the slow cooker and let it sit for 3 hours.

After the 3 hours, remove 2 cups of milk and stir in the half-cup of yogurt in a separate bowl.

Add the yogurt mixture to the remaining milk and stir.

Put the lid back on and wrap in a large and thick bath towel and let sit (unplugged) for an additional 8 hours.

After the 8 hours, unwrap and uncover the slow cooker. SCOOP (DO NOT STIR) the yogurt into clean containers and refrigerate (chill).

Visit our website to watch a how-to video about making homemade yogurt.

11. Easy Yogurt Parfait

PREP 5 MIN

1 cup yogurt

1–2 Tbsp. honey

¼ cup fruit (fresh, canned, or freeze-dried)

¼ cup granola

Instructions

1. Layer in bowl granola, honey, granola and fruit.

2. Serve immediately.

For thick greek yogurt: Pour yogurt into cheesecloth or coffee filter over a bowl or quart jar (allowing the yogurt to drip freely into the bowl or jar as the whey is squeezed out). Cover and place a weight on top (either a bag of water or piece of fruit). Allow whey to drain for 4–8 hours depending on whether you would like Greek yogurt (less thick) or yogurt cheese (like the consistency of a soft cream cheese).

Finding cheesecloth: If you want to get cheesecloth for cheap (much cheaper than you can get at the store), you purchase at Amazon.com. Otherwise, look down the kitchen gadget aisle at your grocery store.

12. *Hashbrown Muffins*

PREP 15 MIN BAKE 25–30 MIN

⅔ cup dehydrated potato shreds, hydrated

¼ cup dehydrated onion flakes, hydrated

1 tsp. salt

2 eggs, beaten (or ½ cup OvaEasy Egg Crystals + ⅔ cup water)

½ cup shredded cheddar cheese

Instructions

1. Heat oven to 375°F. Spray 12 regular-size muffins cups with cooking spray.

2. Place potatoes in large bowl. Add onion and cheese to potatoes in bowl. Stir in beaten eggs and salt.

3. Divide mixture evenly among muffin cups, about ⅓ cup each. Press down into cups.

4. Bake 25 to 30 minutes or until tops are golden brown and crispy.

Optional Mix-ins: Try a can of green chiles, dehydrated peppers, sausage, bacon, or ham to spice things up. Bake 30–40 minutes for 2 loaf recipe, 15–20 minutes for muffins, or 50–60 minutes for one full loaf recipe or until toothpick inserted in center comes out clean.

13. PEACH SMOOTHIE

PREP 5 MIN

2 cups sliced canned peaches

¼ cup peach juice from can

⅔ cup dry milk powder

2 Tbsp. sugar

2 cups crushed ice

Place all of the ingredients in a blender in order listed, cover with a lid, and blend for one minute.

Drinkable Powdered Milk

1 gallon water

3 cups dry milk powder

1 tsp. vanilla, optional

2 Tbsp. sugar, optional

In a one-gallon pitcher, mix 3 cups dry milk powder with ½ gallon water or blend in blender. Add in vanilla and sugar if using (this helps give the milk a sweeter flavor, after all, it's the same trick rice milk uses). Add in last ½ gallon of water and stir. Chill before serving. There is nothing worse than warm powdered milk!

14. BAKED OMELET ROLL

PREP 15 MIN BAKE 20 MIN

6 eggs (⅓ cup dry egg powder + ⅔ cup water)

1 cup milk (3 Tbsp. dry milk powder + 1 cup water)

½ cup all-purpose flour

½ T. salt

¼ T. pepper

1 cup shredded cheddar cheese (or freeze-dried cheese)

Instructions

1. Place eggs and milk in a blender. (or dry powders and water if using food storage items). Add the flour, salt and pepper; cover and process until smooth.

2. Pour into a greased 9×13 pan. bake at 450 for 20 minutes or until eggs are set.

3. Sprinkle with cheese. (If using freeze-dried cheese, begin hydrating once omelet is in the oven by sprinkling with water and stirring until hydrated.)

4. Roll up in pan, starting with a short side. Place with seam side down on a serving platter.

5. Cut into ¾ inch slices.

Extra: Homemade Syrups

Maple Syrup

2 cups sugar (can split 1 cup white sugar and 1 cup brown sugar)

1 cup water

1 Tbsp. corn syrup (helps the syrup to not crystallize)

1 tsp. vanilla

1 tsp. Mapeline maple extract

Boil water and add sugars and corn syrup. Cook until sugar is completely dissolved, about five minutes. Remove from heat and add extracts.

Strawberry Syrup

2 cups strawberries, hulled (or 2 cups freeze-dried strawberries + ¾ cup water)

1 tsp. fresh lemon juice

3 Tbsp. honey or other sweetener

Add to blender and blend until smooth.

Raspberry Syrup

2 cups raspberries (or 2 cups freeze-dried raspberries + ¾ cup water)

1 tsp. fresh lemon juice

¼ cup honey or other sweetener

Add to blender and blend until smooth.

Lunch

2

3

Lunch ideas may seem tricky, but once you learn the tricks to making your family's favorite lunchtime snacks, you'll see it's a breeze to have a normal lunch brought to you by your food storage.

4

5

TRY OUR MOST POPULAR RECIPE FOR A BREAD THAT WILL PASS ANY PEANUT BUTTER AND JELLY TEST! ON PAGE 112

6

7

1. EZ Wheat Bread – pg. 112
This bread is so easy to make and your family will never know it's 100% whole wheat!

2. Homemade Granola Bars – pg. 112
These granola bars are so easy and so cheap–they will leave your family begging for more!

3. Homemade Graham Crackers – pg. 112
Use your food storage to make this kid-friendly favorite!

4. Easy Crackers – pg. 113
Learn our tricks for making delicious homemade crackers, easily!

5. Cheater Fruit Leather – pg. 113
Find out how to use your freeze-dried fruit to make this healthy snack at home.

6. Homemade Go-gurts – pg. 113
Make yogurt healthy again for your kids!

7. Perfectly Popped Popcorn – pg. 113
Popcorn is a great snack! Learn how to pop it with out buying that greasy microwave stuff.

1. EZ Wheat Bread

PREP 20 MIN BAKE 20–30 MIN

1¼ cup warm water

1 Tbsp. active dry yeast

¼ cup honey or ⅓ cup brown sugar

2¾ cups whole wheat flour

¼ cup wheat gluten

1 tsp. salt

2 Tbsp. dry milk powder

1 Tbsp. butter or oil

1 Tbsp. vinegar

¼ cup potato flakes (NOT potato pearls)

Instructions

1. Mix ingredients in order listed in mixing bowl of mixer with dough hook attachment (like kitchen-aid) for 12–15 minutes. Let rise until double, 1–1½ hours. Punch down and shape into loaf or rolls. Let rise again until double and bake 375 degrees for 20–30 minutes until golden brown and sounds hollow when lightly tapped.

2. If using a bread machine, follow its directions for wheat or whole grain selection and add the ingredients in the order listed for their recommendations. (only one loaf will fit in a bread maker).

If using a Bosch mixer, six times this recipe for full capacity.

EZ White Bread

PREP 20 MIN BAKE 20–30 MIN

1⅛ cups warm water

1¾–2 tsp. active dry yeast

2 Tbsp. sugar

3 cups all-purpose or bread flour

1 tsp salt

1 Tbsp. vital wheat gluten (omit if using bread flour)

2 Tbsp. dry milk powder

1½ Tbsp. butter or oil

¼ cup potato flakes

Instructions

1. Mix ingredients in order listed in mixing bowl of mixer with dough hook attachment (like KitchenAid) for 12–15 minutes. Let rise until double, 1–1½ hours. Punch down, and shape into loaf or rolls. Let rise again until double and bake 375 degrees for 20–30 minutes until golden brown and sounds hollow when lightly tapped.

2. If you are making this recipe in a bread machine, follow your bread machine's directions for wheat or whole grain selection and add the ingredients in the order listed for their recommendations. (only one loaf will fit in a bread maker).

If using a Bosch mixer, six times this recipe for full capacity.

Visit our website to watch a how-to video about making homemade bread.

2. HOMEMADE GRANOLA BARS

PREP 10 MIN BAKE 8–10 MIN

1½ cups oats

1 cup crispy rice cereal, crushed pretzel sticks, or any other crispy grain or cereal

½ cup chopped nuts, like walnuts, almonds, peanuts, or pecans

½–1 cup dried fruit, like cranberries, raisins, or cherries

⅓ cup honey

1 tsp. vanilla extract

¼ tsp. salt

½–1 tsp. spices, like cinnamon or pumpkin pie spice (optional)

3 Tbsp. peanut butter or 1 Tbsp. cocoa powder (optional)

Instructions

1. Preheat oven to 325 degrees F. Line the baking pan with parchment, leaving extra parchment to hang over the sides. Lightly coat with nonstick cooking spray. If desired, toast the nuts and grains for 10–15 minutes until toasted and fragrant.

2. Mix the oats, cereal, nuts, and dried fruit together in a bowl. Stir the honey in until the ingredients are completely coated and stick together in clumps. Mix in the vanilla, salt, spices (if using), and peanut butter or cocoa powder (if using).

3. Pour the mixture into the prepared pan. Use wet or lightly oiled hands to firmly press the mixture into the pan.

4. Bake the bars for 20–25 minutes for chewy granola bars or 25–30 minutes for crunchy bars. As soon as you remove the bars from the oven, press them again with the back of a lightly oiled spatula.

5. Let the bars cool completely in the pan. Once cooled, cut into 8 bars in the pan with a very sharp knife, then lift the bars by the flaps of parchment to remove from the pan. Store between layers of wax paper in an airtight container for up to two weeks. To make them easier to slip into backpacks and lunch boxes, you can also wrap each bar individually in wax paper or plastic wrap.

3. HOMEMADE GRAHAM CRACKERS

PREP 15 MIN BAKE 15–20 MIN

2 cups whole wheat flour

¼ cup sugar

½ tsp. salt

1 tsp. cinnamon

1 tsp. baking powder

1 large egg (2 Tbsp. dry egg powder + ¼ cup water)

¼ cup oil

¼ cup honey

2 to 3 Tbsp. milk (1 tsp. dry milk powder + 3 Tbsp. water)

additional milk for glaze

cinnamon-sugar (optional)

Instructions

1. In a mixing bowl, combine whole wheat flour, sugar, salt, cinnamon and baking powder. In a separate bowl, beat egg till light, then add oil, honey and 2 tablespoons milk. Stir into dry ingredients until you have a fairly stiff dough, adding additional milk if necessary. Wrap dough in waxed paper and chill until firm, about 1 hour (or longer, if it's more convenient).

2. Turn the dough onto a floured surface and knead gently until it holds together. Roll dough out till it's about one-sixteenth inches thick; make sure rolling surface is well-floured, or you'll have trouble transferring crackers to baking sheet. Preheat your oven to 375°F.

3. Cut dough into 3-inch squares, prick each square several times with a fork, and place on lightly greased cookie sheets. Brush the tops with milk, sprinkle with cinnamon-sugar if desired, and bake for 15 to 20 minutes, or until crackers are lightly browned. Remove crackers from oven, transfer to a wire cooling rack, and cool completely. Makes about 2 dozen graham crackers.

4. Easy Crackers

PREP 30 MIN BAKE 8–12 MIN

1 cup whole-wheat flour

1 cup all-purpose flour, plus additional for rolling

⅓ cup poppy seeds

⅓ cup sesame seeds

1½ tsp. salt

1½ tsp. baking powder

1 tsp. garlic powder

3 Tbsp. olive oil

¾ cup water

Instructions

1. In a medium bowl whisk together both flours, poppy seeds, sesame seeds, salt, and baking powder. Add the oil and stir until combined. Add the water and stir to combine and create a dough. Turn the dough out onto a floured surface and knead 4 to 5 times. Divide the dough into 8 equal pieces, cover with a tea towel and allow to rest for 15 minutes.

2. Preheat the oven to 450 degrees F.

3. For a thin snacking cracker: On a lightly floured surface, roll out 1 piece of dough to one-sixteenth inch and place on a parchment lined baking sheet. If there is room on the sheet pan, repeat with a second piece of dough. Bake on the middle rack of the oven for 4 minutes then flip and bake for an additional 2 to 3 minutes or until golden brown. Remove from the oven and place on a cooling rack. When cool, break into desired size pieces. Repeat procedure with remaining dough.

For a thicker dipping cracker: On a lightly floured surface, roll out the dough as above but to ⅛-inch thick. Bake for 6 minutes on the first side, then flip and bake another 4 to 6 minutes.

For super even thickness and easy rolling: Roll out using a lightly floured pasta roller. Flatten the dough until it will pass through the first setting and go to the highest number that your pasta roller will allow without tearing the dough. Bake according to the thin cracker instructions.

5. Cheater Fruit Leather

PREP 5 MIN BAKE 3 HOURS

4–4½ cup strawberries (or freeze-dried fruit + ¾ cup water)

½ cup sugar

2 Tbsp lemon juice

Instructions

1. Preheat oven to 170. Line two 12×17 inch rimmed baking sheets with parchment paper.

2. Blend ingredients together until smooth. If desired, strain to remove seeds.

3. Divide mixture between pans, spread evenly. Bake for 3 hours or until leather is no longer sticky. Rotate pans 180 degrees and swapping levels half way through.

4. Using kitchen scissors, cut leather into strips. Roll up and store in an airtight container.

6. HOMEMADE GO-GURTS

PREP 15 MIN FREEZE 1–2 HOURS

1 cup flavored yogurt

2 Tbsp. skim milk

Instructions

1. Blend yogurt, milk, and any additional ingredients.

2. Pour into tubes.

3. Refrigerate or freeze 6 hours or overnight until frozen.

Flavor options:

Here are some ideas to get you going, but it is also really fun for kids to make their own flavor concoctions.

ORANGE: Replace 2 tablespoons skim milk with orange juice

FRESH PEACHES & CREAM: 1 teaspoon vanilla extract and ½ peach peeled and diced

FRESH STRAWBERRY: 4 strawberries, diced, and ½ kiwi, diced

CHOCOLATE: Using double batch (2 cups), add 1 (3-oz.) package of chocolate instant pudding

VANILLA: Using double batch (2 cups), add 1 (3-oz.) package of vanilla instant pudding

You can also dice 1–2 bananas to add to the chocolate and vanilla variations.

Disposable bags (like those pictured on the right) and reusable silicon molds are available for purchase at Amazon.com

7. PERFECTLY POPPED POPCORN

PREP 2 MIN COOK 10 MIN

3 Tbsp. coconut, peanut, or canola oil (high smoke point oil)

⅓ cup of high quality popcorn kernels

1 Tbsp. or more (to taste) of butter (optional)

Salt to taste

Instructions

1. Heat the oil in a 3-quart saucepan on medium high heat. If you are using coconut oil, allow all of the solid oil to melt perfect.

2. Put 3 or 4 popcorn kernels into the oil and cover the pan.

3. When the kernels pop, add the rest of the ⅓ cup of popcorn kernels in an even layer. Cover, remove from heat and count 30 seconds. (Count out loud; it's fun to do with kids.)

4. Return the pan to the heat. The popcorn should begin popping soon, and all at once. Once the popping starts in earnest, gently shake the pan by moving it back and forth over the burner. Try to keep the lid slightly ajar to let the steam from the popcorn release (the popcorn will be drier and crisper).

5. Once the popping slows to several seconds between pops, remove the pan from the heat, remove the lid, and dump the popcorn immediately into a wide bowl. With this technique, nearly all of the kernels pop, and nothing burns.

Dinner
WEEK ONE

SUNDAY

2

MONDAY

3

TUESDAY

Dinner doesn't have to be bland just because you're using food storage. It can still be full of your family's favorites, classic dishes, savory soups, and budget-friendly beans and rice.

LEARN HOW TO MAKE OUR EASY SANDWICH ROLLS ON PAGE 116

4

WEDNESDAY

5

THURSDAY

6

FRIDAY

7

SATURDAY

1. *Thanksgiving Casserole* – pg. 116
All of your holiday favorites wrapped up into one delicious casserole!

2. *Black Bean Burgers* – pg. 116
Satisfy your cravings with these hearty burgers.

3. *Easy Spaghetti* – pg. 116
It's so easy your kids could make it!

4. *Cajun Red Beans & Rice* – pg. 117
Beans and rice don't have to be bland as anyone from New Orleans will tell you!

5. *Tuna Fish Casserole* – pg. 117
This classic dish gets a food storage makeover.

6. *Easy Tamale Pie* – pg. 117
Make it a fiesta with this no fuss pie.

7. *Roasted Tomato & Barley Soup* – pg. 117
Food storage turns gourmet with this delicious, easy soup.

1. *Thanksgiving Casserole*

PREP 15 MIN BAKE 30 MIN

3 cups prepared mashed potatoes (1½ cups potato pearls + 3 cups hot water)

2 (12-ounce) cans turkey or chicken chunks, drained (or 1 pint bottled, drained) reserve liquid for gravy

2 (0.07-ounce) packages chicken gravy mix

1 (15-ounce) can mixed vegetable or equivalent, drained*

1 (6-ounce) box Stove Top stuffing mix mixed with 1½ c. hot water

Instructions

1. Spread mashed potatoes in bottom of 9×13 casserole. Distribute meat and vegetables over potatoes.

2. Prepare gravy according to labeled directions using the reserved liquid (this is actually broth and will add extra flavor to your gravy) from the chicken cans. Use water for the rest of the required liquid. Spread the gravy evenly on top of potatoes and vegetables.

3. Top with stuffing and bake at 350 degrees for 30 minutes, until heated through.

4. Serve with cranberry sauce if desired.

You can reserve the liquid from the can of vegetables and use it towards the water needed to make the mashed potatoes or stuffing.

2. BLACK BEAN BURGERS

PREP 10 MIN COOK 8 MIN

½ onion, diced (or ¼ cup dehydrated onions, hydrated)

1 (15-ounce) can black beans, well drained (or 1¾ cup cooked black beans-roughly ½ cup dry beans cooked)

½ cup flour

2 slices bread, crumbled

1 tsp. garlic powder

1 tsp. onion powder

½ tsp. seasoned salt

salt and pepper to taste

oil for frying

Instructions

1. Sauté the onions till soft, about 3–5 minutes. Unless you're using hydrated onions and then you can skip this step.

2. In a large bowl, mash the beans until almost smooth. Add sauteed onions and the rest of the ingredients, except the oil, adding the flour a few tablespoons at a time to combine well. Mixture will be thick.

3. Form bean mixture into patties, approximately ½ inch thick and fry patties in a small amount of oil until slightly firm.

4. Serve on our 40-minute hamburger buns with Chipotle Mayo and fresh tomato and lettuce from the garden, if available.

Chipotle Mayo

½ cup mayo

2 chipotle chilies in adobo sauce from 1 (7-ounce) can of chipotles

1 Tbsp. adobo sauce from chipotle peppers

Instructions

1. Thoroughly combine all ingredients until well blended.

40-minute Hamburger Buns

PREP 30 MIN BAKE 8–12 MIN

2 Tbsp. active dry yeast

1 cup plus 2 tablespoons warm water (110° to 115°)

⅓ cup vegetable oil

¼ cup sugar

1 egg (1 Tbsp. dry egg powder + NO water)*

1 tsp. salt

3 to 3½ cups all-purpose flour

Instructions

1. In a large mixer bowl, dissolve yeast in warm water. Add oil and sugar; let stand for 5 minutes.

2. Add the egg, salt and enough flour to form a soft dough.

3. Knead until smooth and elastic, about 3–5 minutes.

4. Do not let rise. Divide into 12 pieces; shape each into a ball. Place 3 inches apart on greased baking sheets.

5. Cover and let rest for 10 minutes. Bake at 425° for 8–12 minutes or until golden brown. Remove from pans to wire racks to cool. Yield: 1 dozen.

We've learned that when you're using powdered eggs in bread, no extra water is necessary. In fact, the extra water can make the dough sticky!

3. EASY SPAGHETTI

PREP 5 MIN COOK 15 MIN

Spaghetti can be as simple as your favorite jar or can of spaghetti sauce and a package of noodles. But if you'd like to try our super simple spaghetti sauce instead of the store bought stuff, go right ahead!

1 (15-ounce) can diced tomatoes

1 (15-ounce) can tomato sauce

1 (6-ounce) can tomato paste

2 Tbsp. sugar (optional)

½ tsp. basil

½ tsp. oregano

½ tsp. black pepper

½ tsp. salt

1 tsp. crushed red pepper flakes (optional)

Instructions

1. Mix all ingredients in a sauce pan. Stir, simmer, cover, and continue to simmer for 20–30 minutes.

2. Season again to taste.

3. Serve over hot noodles.

4. CAJUN RED BEANS & RICE

PREP 5 MIN   COOK 4–5 HOURS

1 lb. dry red kidney beans, rinsed and sorted

6 cups water

5 chicken or ham bouillon cubes

1 onion, chopped (½ cup dehydrated onions)

4–5 cloves garlic, minced

1 tsp. Cajun or Creole seasoning (Tony Chachere's is the best)

¾ tsp. cumin

¾ tsp. coriander

¾ tsp. oregano

⅛-¼ tsp. cinnamon

½ tsp. smoked paprika

Instructions

1. Combine all ingredients in a slow cooker and cook on high for 4–5 hours or on low all day.

2. When beans are tender, mash about 85–90% of them against the side of the slow cooker. Taste them and add any extra seasonings if you need to, particularly more Tony's or salt and pepper. Replace lid and set heat to "low."

3. In a medium saucepan, bring 4 cups water, 1 Tbsp. white vinegar, and 2 cups of white rice to a boil. Reduce heat to low, cover, and steam for 20 minutes.

4. Serve beans with rice.

5. *Tuna Fish Casserole*

PREP 15 MIN   COOK 20 MIN

1 (10½-ounce) can Condensed Cream of Celery Soup

½ cup milk (1½ Tbsp. dry milk powder + ½ cup water)

1 cup freeze-dried green peas, hydrated

2 cans (about 5 ounces each) tuna in water, drained

4 ounces (about 2 cups) medium egg noodles, cooked and drained

2 tablespoons dry bread crumbs

1 tablespoon oil

Instructions

1. Heat the oven to 400°F. Stir the soup, milk, peas, tuna and noodles in a 1½-quart baking dish. Stir the bread crumbs and oil in a small bowl.

2. Bake for 20 minutes or until the tuna mixture is hot and bubbling. Stir the tuna mixture. Sprinkle with the bread crumb mixture.

3. Bake for 5 additional minutes or until the bread crumb mixture is golden brown.

6. *Easy Tamale Pie*

PREP 15 MIN   COOK 6–8 HOURS

1 pound ground beef, cooked (or 1 pint jar ground beef, drained)

1 tsp. ground cumin

1 tsp. chili powder

½ tsp. salt

¼ tsp. pepper

1 (15-ounce) can black beans, rinsed and drained (1¾ cup cooked black beans-roughly ½ cup dry beans cooked)

1 (14½-ounce) can diced tomatoes, undrained

1 (11-ounce) can whole kernel corn, drained

1 (10-ounce) can enchilada sauce

½ cup onion (¼ cup dehydrated onions)

1 (8½-ounce) package corn bread/muffin mix

2 eggs, lightly beaten (2 Tbsp. dry egg powder + ¼ cup water)

1 cup (4 ounces) shredded cheddar (1 cup freeze-dried cheese, hydrated), optional

Instructions

1. Combine beef and seasonings.

2. Transfer to a 4-qt. slow cooker. Stir in beans, tomatoes, corn, enchilada sauce, and onions. Cook, covered, on low 6–8 hours or until heated through.

3. In a small bowl, combine muffin mix and eggs; spoon over beef mixture. Cook, covered, on low 1 to 1½ hours longer or until a toothpick inserted in corn bread layer comes out clean.

4. Sprinkle with cheese; let stand, covered, 5 minutes.

7. ROASTED TOMATO & BARLEY SOUP

PREP 35 MIN   COOK 35 MIN

2 (14.5-ounce) cans diced tomatoes, drained, reserving juice

2 large onions, diced (or ¾ cup dehydrated onions, hydrated)

2 cloves garlic, minced

2 tablespoons olive oil

4 cubes chicken broth

4 cups water

2 stalks celery, diced (or ½ cup dehydrated or 1 cup freeze-dried celery)

½ cup uncooked pearl barley

1 Tbsp. dry parsley

Instructions

1. Heat the oven to 425°F. Place the tomatoes, onions and garlic into a large roasting pan. Drizzle the oil over the vegetables and toss to coat. Roast for 25 minutes.

2. Place the vegetables into a 3-quart saucepan. Stir in the reserved tomato juice, broth, celery, and barley and heat to a boil. Reduce the heat to low. Cover and cook for 35 minutes or until the barley is tender. Stir in the parsley.

Dinner
WEEK TWO

SUNDAY

9

MONDAY

10
TUESDAY

LEARN HOW TO MAKE DELICIOUS HOMEMADE NOODLES ON PAGE 134

NO NEED TO BE AFRAID OF MAKING HOMEMADE TORTILLAS. LEARN OUR BEST TRICKS ON PAGE 121

11
WEDNESDAY

12

THURSDAY

13
FRIDAY

14

SATURDAY

8. *Beef & Gravy Mashed Potatoes* – pg. 120
Make this Sunday comfort meal in minutes using our food storage tricks.

9. *Lentil Sloppy Joes* – pg. 120
No need to be fearful of the title, these are kid tested and mother approved!

10. *Fettuccine Alfredo* – pg. 120
Make this easy dish in under 20 minutes.

11. *Puerto Rican Rice & Beans* – pg. 120
Beans and rice will quickly become your favorite after you try this recipe.

12. *Skillet Beef & Mac* – pg. 120
Your kids are sure to love this classic recipe.

13. *Slow Cooker Bean & Rice Wraps* – pg. 121
Make these easy and delicious burritos in a snap.

14. *Kid's Favorite Chili* – pg. 121
Chili is a wonderful food storage dish.

8. *Beef & Gravy over Mashed Potatoes*

PREP 5 MIN COOK 15 MIN

1 pound (or 1 pint) cubed beef

1 (10¾ ounce) can condensed cream of mushroom soup

2 (4-ounce) cans sliced mushrooms, drained

1 (1-ounce) package dry onion soup mix

3 cups prepared mashed potatoes (1½ cups potato pearls + 3 cups hot water)

Instructions

1. In a 3½-quart saucepan, combine beef, soup, mushrooms, and soup mix. Cook over medium heat until warmed through. Serve over prepared mashed potatoes.

9. LENTIL SLOPPY JOES

PREP 5 MIN COOK 30 MIN

¾ cup brown lentils

2 cups water

2 medium onions chopped, (or ½ cup dehydrated onions)

1 (10½-ounce) can condensed tomato soup

½ cup ketchup

2 Tbsp. brown sugar

1½ tsp. chili powder

1½ tsp. Worcestershire sauce

1 tsp. salt

1½ tsp. dry mustard

½ tsp. curry powder

hamburger buns

Instructions

1. Rinse lentils. Combine lentils and water in a 2 qt. saucepan. Bring water to a rapid simmer on medium-high heat, then reduce heat to a simmer. Cook uncovered from 20–30 minutes. Drain lentils using a colander.

2. While lentil are cooking, mix together all ingredients remaining ingredients except hamburger buns and simmer for 20–30 minutes.

3. Combine lentils and sauce and spoon over hamburger buns.

10. FETTUCCINE ALFREDO

PREP 4 MIN COOK 15 MIN

1 (15-ounce) jar Alfredo pasta sauce

1 package (8 oz.) fettuccine pasta

Instructions

1. Cook pasta al dente according to package instructions and drain.

2. Combine sauce and pasta in sauce pan and warm for 4–6 minutes, or until heated through, stirring occasionally. Serve immediately.

11. PUERTO RICAN RICE & BEANS

PREP 5 MIN COOK 15 MIN

¼ cup olive oil

¼ cup GOYA® Sofrito

2 packets GOYA® Sazón without Annatto

1 cube chicken bouillon

1 cup water

¼ tsp. Oregano

1 (8-ounce) can tomato sauce

2 (15½-ounce) cans pinto or pink beans drained and rinsed (or 3½ cups cooked pinto or pink beans—roughly 1 cup dry beans cooked)

2 cups cooked rice prepared according to package directions

Instructions

1. Heat oil in 4-qt. saucepan over medium-high heat. Add sofrito, sazón, bouillon, and oregano. Cook until vegetable mixture becomes soft and fragrant, 1–2 minutes. Add ½ cup water, beans and tomato sauce to vegetable mixture. Bring water to a boil; reduce heat to medium low and simmer, stirring occasionally, until flavors come together and bean mixture becomes thick, about 15 minutes.

2. Divide rice evenly among serving plates. Serve seasoned beans on top or alongside rice.

12. *Skillet Beef & Mac*

PREP 5 MIN COOK 15 MIN

1 pound ground beef (or 1 pint ground beef, drained)

2 stalks celery, diced (or ½ cup dehydrated or 1 cup freeze-dried celery, hydrated)

½ tsp. dried oregano

1 (10½-ounce) can Cream of Mushroom Soup

1 cup prepared picante salsa

1 (8-ounce) can whole kernel corn, drained

4 ounces (about 1 cup) elbow macaroni, cooked and drained

¼ cup shredded freeze-dried cheddar cheese, hydrated

Instructions

1. Cook or warm the beef, celery, and oregano in a 10-inch skillet over medium-high heat until the beef is well browned, stirring often to separate meat. Pour off any fat.

2. Stir the soup, picante salsa, corn, and pasta in the skillet. Cook and stir until the mixture is hot and bubbling. Sprinkle with the cheese and cook until the cheese is melted.

13. SLOW COOKER BEAN & RICE WRAPS

PREP 5 MIN   COOK 15 MIN

1 (10½-ounce) can nacho cheese

1 (15½-ounce) can corn, drained reserving liquid

1 (15½-ounce) can diced tomatoes, drained reserving liquid

2 (15½-ounce) cans (15.5 oz) pinto beans drained and rinsed (or 3½ cups cooked pinto beans-roughly 1 cup dry beans cooked)

1 tsp. taco seasoning

1 cup rice, prepared

tortillas

Instructions

1. Combine nacho cheese, corn, tomatoes, beans and taco seasoning and heat through.

2. Prepare 1 cup of rice using reserved liquid from corn and tomatoes and needed water.

3. Layer rice and bean mixture on top of tortillas. (If you don't have tortillas, you can always serve this recipe with just the beans and rice. But be sure to double the rice if you are omitting tortillas.)

This is why using canned food is so great: you can always use the liquid from your cans in your recipes to hydrate or cook other food!

Easy Tortillas

PREP 20 MIN   COOK 10 MIN

3 cups flour

1 teaspoon salt

1 teaspoon baking powder

⅓ cup vegetable oil

1 cup warm water

Instructions

1. Combine flour, salt and baking powder in the bowl of a stand mixer. With the dough hook attached mix dry ingredients until well combined. Add oil and water with mixer running at a medium speed. Mix for 1 minute, stopping several times to scrape the sides of the bowl. After about 1 minute, or when mixture comes together and begins to form a ball, decrease mixing speed to low. Continue to mix for 1 minute or until dough is smooth.

2. Transfer from mixing bowl to a well-floured work surface. Divide dough in half, then in half again. Continue until you have 8 fairly equal portions. Form each piece into a ball and flatten with the palm of your hand as much as possible. If dough is sticky, use a bit more flour. Cover flattened balls of dough with a clean kitchen towel and allow to rise for 15 minutes before proceeding.

3. After rest period, heat a large pan over medium-high heat. Roll each dough piece into a rough circle, about 10–12 inches in diameter, keep work surface and rolling pin lightly floured. Don't stack uncooked tortillas on top of each other or they will get soggy.

4. When pan is very hot, place one dough circle into pan and allow to cook about 1 minute or until bottom surface has a few pale brown spots. The uncooked surface will begin to show a few little bubbles. If tortilla is browning too fast, reduced heat a bit. If it's taking longer than a minute to see a few pale golden brown spots on underside of tortillas, increase heat a bit. Flip to other side and cook for about 30 seconds. You want the tortilla to be soft but have a few small pale golden brown spots on surface. Remove from pan with tongs and stack in a covered container or zippered bag till all tortillas are cooked. This will keep them soft and pliable.

5. Wipe out the pan in between tortillas if flour is starting to accumulate. Serve warm or allow to cool for later use. When ready to use, place a slightly damp paper towel in the bottom of a container (with a cover) that will hold the stacked tortillas. Microwave, uncovered for 15–25 seconds (start with 15) or until warm, then cover to hold heat while serving.

6. The tortillas will keep well stored in an airtight container or zippered bag at room temperature for 24 hours or can be frozen indefinitely. To freeze, separate tortillas with parchment paper or waxed paper and place in a zippered bag before placing in freezer.

14. KID'S FAVORITE CHILI

PREP 10 MIN   COOK 1 HOUR

2 (15¾ ounce) cans red kidney beans (or 3 cups dry red beans cooked)

1 (8-ounce) can tomato sauce

1 (15½-ounce) can diced tomatoes

1½ cup ketchup

¼ cup lemon juice

¼ cup brown sugar (or ¼ cup sugar + 1 tsp. molasses)

1 cup celery, coarsely chopped (or ½ cup dehydrated or 1 cup freeze-dried celery)

1 cup onion, coarsely chopped (or ½ cup dehydrated onions)

1 small bay leaf

1 Tbsp. chili powder

1½ tsp. salt

½ tsp. dry mustard

2 Tbsp. Worcestershire sauce

1 pound ground beef (or 1 pint ground beef)

Instructions

Combine ingredients. Cover and simmer 1 hour. If you used dehydrated or freeze-dried vegetables, do not hydrate. They will hydrate as they simmer in the chili. The longer it cooks, the thicker it becomes and the better it tastes—add water as needed.

Dinner
WEEK THREE

SUNDAY

16

MONDAY

17

TUESDAY

LEARN HOW TO MAKE ARTISAN BREAD IN JUST A FEW MINUTES A DAY WITH ONLY THREE INGREDIENTS ON PAGE 124

WHETHER YOU'RE IN A RUSH OR ARE PLANNING AHEAD, THERE ARE MANY DIFFERENT OPTIONS FOR COOKING YOUR BEANS ON PAGE 53

18

WEDNESDAY

19

THURSDAY

20

FRIDAY

21

SATURDAY

15. Chicken Pot Pie

PREP 10 MIN **BAKE** 30 MIN

1 (15½-ounce) can mixed vegetables

1 pint chicken, drained

1 (10¾-ounce) can condensed cream of chicken soup

1 cup biscuit mix

½ cup milk (or 1½ Tbsp. dry milk powder + ½ cup water)

1 egg (or 1 Tbsp. dry egg powder + 2 Tbsp. water)

Instructions

1. Heat oven to 400 degrees F. Mix vegetables, chicken and soup in ungreased glass pie plate, 9×1¼ inches.

2. Stir together remaining ingredients with fork until blended. Pour into pie plate.

3. Bake 30 minutes or until golden brown.

16. Black Bean and Corn Empanadas

PREP 35 MIN **BAKE** 25 MIN

Empanada Dough

2 cups flour

½ tsp. salt

⅓ cup white sugar

1 egg yolk (or 1 Tbsp. dry egg powder)

½ cup water

2 Tbsp. flour for dusting

2 Tbsp. oil or butter or oil for brushing

Instructions

1. Pre-heat oven to 400 degrees.

2. Whisk together the flour, salt, and sugar in a bowl until evenly blended; make a well in the center of the mixture. Whisk the egg yolk and water together in a small bowl until smooth; pour into the well and mix to form a stiff dough. Transfer the dough to a lightly floured surface and knead until smooth and elastic, about 8 minutes.

3. Cut dough into eight equal pieces. On a lightly floured surface, roll each piece of dough into a (roughly) 6" round. Mound a spoonful of filling into the center of each dough round. Fold the dough over the mound, forming a half-circle.

4. Pinch, fold, or crimp the edge of the dough to seal.

5. Brush the tops with the melted butter or oil.

6. Place the prepared empanadas on a lined baking sheet (either parchment paper or baking mat). Place the baking sheet into the preheated oven and bake for 25 minutes, or until the pastry is light, golden brown.

Filling

1 (15-ounce) can black beans, drained and rinsed (or 1 ¾ cup cooked black beans-roughly ½ cup dry beans cooked)

1 (15-ounce) can corn, drained

1 cup grated mozzarella cheese

1 (4-ounce) can green chilies

½ cup diced sweet bell peppers (or ¼ cup dehydrated or ½ cup freeze-dried peppers)

½ cup salsa

¼ cup diced onion (or 2 Tbsp. dehydrated onions)

½ tsp. ground cumin

½ tsp. dry cilantro

½ tsp. kosher salt

¼ tsp. ground coriander

Instructions

1. Place all of the ingredients into a large bowl and stir to combine.

17. EASIER THAN EASY GNOCCHI

PREP 15 MIN **COOK** 10 MIN

1 cup dry potato flakes

1 cup boiling water

1 egg, beaten (or 1 Tbsp. dry egg powder + 2 Tbsp. water)

1 tsp. salt

⅛ tsp. ground black pepper

1½ cups flour

Instructions

1. Place potato flakes in a medium-size bowl. Pour in boiling water; stir until blended. Let cool.

2. Stir in egg, salt, and pepper. Blend in enough flour to make a fairly stiff dough.

3. Turn dough out on a well floured board. Knead lightly.

4. Divide dough in half. Shape each half into a long thin roll, the thickness of a breadstick. With a knife dipped in flour, cut into bite-size pieces.

5. Place a few gnocchi in boiling water. As the gnocchi rise to the top of the pot, remove them with a slotted spoon. Repeat until all are cooked.

6. Serve with bottled alfredo or spaghetti sauce.

Artisan Bread

PREP 30 MIN **BAKE** 8–12 MIN

3 cups flour

½ tsp. instant or rapid rise yeast

1¾ tsp. kosher salt

1½ cups cool tap water

Instructions

1. In a large mixing bowl, mix the yeast in ¼ cup warm water. Add flour and salt. Pour in 1 ½ cups water and mix the dough together. In a large mixing bowl add 3 cups all-purpose flour. Add ½ teaspoon instant yeast.

2. Using a wooden spoon or rubber spatula mix the dough, but remember it is a "NO-knead" bread. Cover the bowl with plastic wrap.

3. Let the dough sit for at least 3–4 hours at room temperature or longer in your refrigerator. If you put it in the refrigerator cover it loosely with a lid.

4. Heavily flour a surface. Don't worry about large air bubbles—it's artisan bread and you will want the large air holes. Form a loaf and place on a pan covered with cornmeal. Cover with plastic wrap and let sit for 30 minutes to rise. Twenty minutes before you need to bake the bread, pre-heat oven to 450 degrees.

5. Slash loaf just before baking.

6. Turn your oven into a steam oven by placing a large broiler pan of boiling water on the bottom shelf just before putting the bread in the oven. Close the door quickly and do not open again! Creating a steam oven will create a wonderful crispy texture to the crust of your bread.

18. CUBAN BEANS & RICE

PREP 15 MIN COOK 30–40 MIN

1 cup rice

1 cup coconut milk

1½ cups chicken broth

¼ tsp. salt

¼ tsp. pepper

1 Tbsp. oil

½ large onion, chopped (or ¼ cup dehydrated onions, hydrated)

2 (15½ ounce) cans black beans drained and rinsed (or 3½ cups cooked black beans-roughly 1 cup dry beans cooked)

2 tsp. chili powder

⅛ tsp. cayenne

1 cup chicken broth

¼ cup lime juice

¾ cup chopped cilantro (you can use ¼ cup dried cilantro, but fresh from your garden is best)

1 cup toasted coconut, optional

Instructions

1. Bring coconut milk, 1½ cups chicken broth, salt, and pepper to a boil in a 2-quart saucepan. Add rice and bring back to a boil, stirring constantly. Cover, then reduce heat and simmer for 20–25 minutes.

2. In a pot, sauté onions in oil until soft. Add beans, chili powder, cayenne, and 1 cup chicken broth. Bring to a boil, then reduce heat and simmer for 10–15 minutes, adding more broth if the beans are too dry.

3. Place cooked rice and beans, lime juice, cilantro, and coconut in serving dish and mix well.

19. Creamy Beef & Noodles

PREP 10 MIN COOK 10 MIN

1 pound beef (or 1 pint cooked beef chunks, reserve liquid and use towards beef broth)

1 dash ground black pepper

1 (10½ ounce) can condensed cream of mushroom soup

1 ¾ cups beef broth (or 2 cubes beef bouillon + 1¾ cups water)

½ cup water

1 cup onion, diced (or ½ cup dehydrated onions-no need to hydrate)

4 ounces (⅓ of a 12-ounce package) uncooked egg noodles

½ cup plain yogurt

Instructions

1. Season the beef with the black pepper. Cook or warm the beef in a 12-inch nonstick skillet over medium-high heat until it's well

browned, stirring often. Remove the beef from the skillet. Pour off any fat.

2. Stir the soup, broth, water, and onion in the skillet and heat to a boil. Stir in the noodles. Reduce the heat to medium and cook for 10 minutes or until the noodles are tender, stirring often.

3. Stir the yogurt in the skillet. Return the beef to the skillet. Cook until the mixture is hot and bubbling, stirring often. Sprinkle with the parsley, if desired.

*See page 134 for *Homemade Noodle* recipe

20. Mexican Lasagna

PREP 10 MIN BAKE 30 MIN

1 (10½-ounce) can condensed cream of mushroom soup

½ cup non fat milk (or 1½ Tbsp. dry milk powder + ½ cup water)

¾ pound ground beef (or 1 pint cooked ground beef, drained)

1 medium onion, chopped (or ¼ cup dehydrated onions, hydrated)

1 Tbsp. chili powder

1 (10¾-ounce) can condensed tomato soup

4 lasagna noodles, cooked without salt and drained

½ cup shredded cheddar cheese (or ½ cup freeze-dried cheese, hydrated)

Instructions

1. Stir the mushroom soup and milk in a small bowl until the mixture is smooth.

2. Cook (or warm, if you're using canned beef) the beef, onion and chili powder in a 3-quart saucepan over medium-high heat until the beef is well browned, stirring often to separate meat. Pour off any fat.

3. Stir the tomato soup in the saucepan and cook until the mixture is hot and bubbling.

4. Layer half the beef mixture, 2 lasagna noodles and half the mushroom soup mixture in an 8-inch square baking dish, trimming the noodles to fit the dish, if needed. Repeat the layers. Sprinkle with the cheese.

5. Bake at 400°F. for 30 minutes or until the filling is hot and the cheese is melted. Let stand for 10 minutes before serving.

21. Mac 'n' Cheese Soup

PREP 5 MIN COOK 15 MIN

1 (7¼-ounce) box macaroni and cheese

3½ cups water

¼ cup dehydrated onions

1 cup chopped frozen broccoli (or 1 cup freeze-dried broccoli)

1 (10¾-ounce) can condensed cheese soup

2½ cup milk (or heaping ⅓ cup dry non-instant milk + 2½ cups water)

1 cup cubed Spam

Instructions

1. Cook macaroni and onion in water for 6½ minutes.

2. Add in broccoli and cook for another 1–2 minute. Or if you are using the freeze-dried broccoli add for 30 seconds.

3. Add remaining ingredients (including the cheese packet from your box of macaroni and cheese) and warm through. (If you're using powdered milk, combine the powder and water before adding or you'll have clumpy soup.) If the soup is too thick, simply add in water to desired consistency.

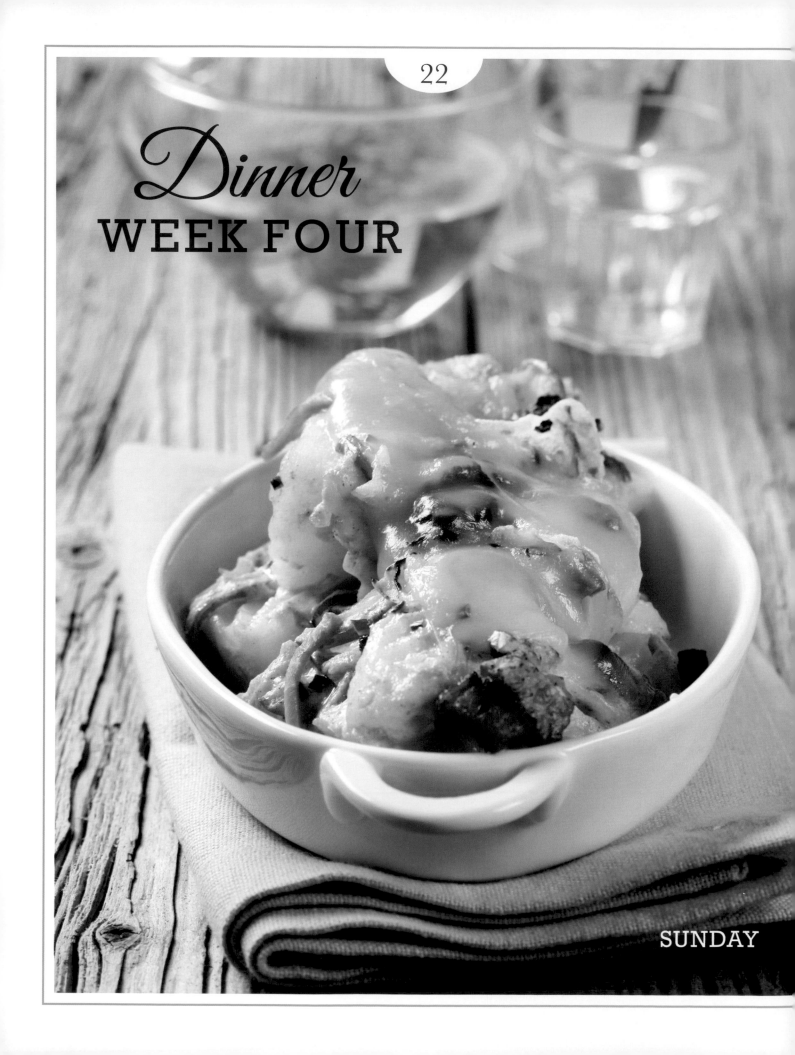

Dinner
WEEK FOUR

SUNDAY

23

MONDAY

24

TUESDAY

MAKE PIZZA, CALZONE, OR BREADSTICK DOUGH IN UNDER 30 MINUTES!

LEARN HOW TO MAKE SWEETENED CONDENSED AND EVAPORATED MILK FROM YOUR POWDERED MILK ON PAGE 134

25

WEDNESDAY

26

THURSDAY

27

FRIDAY

28

SATURDAY

22. Scalloped Potatoes & Ham – pg. 128
This cheesy dish is a must for any one-dish supper.

23. Tuna Fish Sandwich – pg. 128
Whether you like it hot or cold, this sandwich is sure to satisfy.

24. Calzones – pg. 128
Make calzones instead of pizza to allow your family to make it just how they like it.

25. Indian Red Bean Curry – pg. 128
These savory beans and rice are sure to please even the pickiest eaters.

26. Chicken Rice & Broccoli Casserole – pg. 129
A wonderfully satisfying one-dish meal.

27. Chipotle Tortilla Soup – pg. 129
You'll feel like you're eating at a popular restaurant when you try this recipe.

28. Garlic Potato Soup – pg. 129
A delicious creamy soup made with out the cream.

22. Scalloped Potatoes & Ham

PREP 10 MIN **COOK** 30–35 MIN

1 (4.7-ounce) box Betty Crocker™ au gratin potatoes

2⅓ cups hot water

⅔ cup milk

½ cup frozen peas (or ½ cup freeze-dried peas)

1 (12-ounce) can of Spam or ham, chopped

½ cup shredded cheddar cheese (2 ounces), or freeze-dried cheese, rehydrated

Instructions

1. Stir together potatoes, sauce mix, hot water, and milk in 10-inch skillet; stir in peas until separated.

2. Heat to boiling; reduce heat. Cover and simmer 25 minutes, stirring occasionally, until potatoes are tender.

3. Stir in ham; cover and heat 3 to 4 minutes or just until ham is hot. Sprinkle cheese over mixture. Cover; let stand about 5 minutes or until cheese is melted.

23. Tuna Fish Sandwich

PREP 10 MIN

Makes about 2 cups of salad

2 (5-ounce) cans water-packed tuna fish, drained

2 to 4 Tbsp. mayonnaise

2 Tbsp. mustard

1 rib celery, diced small (or 2 Tbsp. dehydrated celery, allow to hydrate in salad)

1 Tbsp. pickle relish, optional

salt and pepper

Instructions

1. Add mayonnaise, mustard, celery, pickle relish (if using), a sprinkle of salt, and a few cracks of fresh black pepper to the tuna fish. Stir with a fork to combine, breaking up any large chunks of tuna fish as you go. Add more mayo if you'd like smoother, creamier tuna salad. Taste and add more of any of the ingredients to taste.

2. Use immediately or store in a covered container in the refrigerator for up to a week.

TUNA SALAD VARIATIONS

- Use greek yogurt instead of mayo for a lighter salad
- Use canned salmon, smoked trout, or leftover chicken in place of the tuna
- Add diced apples, raisins, or dried fruit to the basic recipe. Omit mustard and relish if adding fruit

24. Calzones

PREP 30 MIN **BAKE** 10–15 MIN

2½ cups medium hot water

2 Tbsp. yeast

2 Tbsp. sugar

3 Tbsp. oil

1 tsp. salt

6 cups flour (you can do half all-purpose and half whole wheat or 100% whole wheat)

1½ cup pizza sauce (see recipe below)

1 (15½-ounce) can olives, drained and sliced

2 (4-ounce) cans mushrooms, drained

2½ cups shredded mozzarella cheese or 2½ cups freeze-dried mozzarella cheese, hydrated

2 Tbsp. oil, melted

Instructions

1. Pour medium hot water in mixing bowl. Sprinkle yeast on top and allow to dissolve. Add sugar, salt, and oil. Gradually add approximately 6 cups of flour.

2. Allow dough to rise until it has doubled in size (about 10–15 minutes). Divide dough into 8 equal sections and roll into circles.

3. Top with sauce, cheese and desired toppings (olives and mushrooms). Fold circles over and seal edges. Brush with oil, if desired.

4. Bake at 350 degrees F (175 degrees C) for 10–15 minutes, or until brown on top.

Use the bread recipe above for quick and easy breadsticks or pizza dough!

Pizza Sauce

1 (15-ounce) can tomato sauce

1 (6-ounce) can tomato paste

1 Tbsp. ground oregano

1½ tsp. dried minced garlic

1 tsp. ground paprika

Instructions

1. In a medium bowl, Mix together tomato sauce and tomato paste until smooth. Stir in oregano, garlic, and paprika.

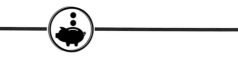

25. INDIAN RED BEAN CURRY

PREP 10 MIN **COOK** 10 MIN

⅓ cup extra-virgin olive oil

¼ cup chopped fresh ginger (or 2 Tbsp. ground ginger, but really fresh is best)

1 cup onion, finely chopped (or ⅓ cup dehydrated onion)

1 plum tomato, diced, or ⅓ cup diced canned tomatoes

3 cloves garlic, chopped

1 tsp. salt

1 tsp. ground cumin

1 tsp. ground coriander

½ tsp. cumin seeds

½ tsp. ground turmeric

¼ tsp. cayenne

1 (8-ounce) can of tomato sauce

3 cups boiled red kidney beans or 30 ounces canned red kidney beans, undrained

½ cup chopped fresh cilantro (or ¼ cup dried cilantro)

3 cups prepared rice

Instructions

1. Heat oil in a deep sauce pan over medium heat for one minute. Add ginger, garlic, onion, and let sizzle for one minute. Add the tomato sauce, salt, and remaining spices and cook for an additional five minutes, stirring frequently.

2. Add the kidney beans with water or canned red kidney beans (undrained) plus one additional cup of water, and tomatoes. Bring it to a boil, then reduce to medium heat and let cook uncovered for 10 minutes. Remove from heat. Garnish with cilantro.

3. Serve over rice. A dollop of plain yogurt on top is heavenly.

26. *Chicken, Rice & Broccoli Casserole*

PREP 10 MIN   BAKE 30–35 MIN

2 cups cooked chicken or 2 pints cooked chicken (or 2 cups freeze-dried chicken)

2 cups broccoli florets, (or 2 cups freeze-dried broccoli) broken down into bite-sized pieces

1 (10¾-ounce) can cream of chicken soup

2 cups cooked rice

1½ cups shredded cheese (or 1½ cups freeze-dried shredded cheese, hydrated)

½ cup mayonnaise

½–¾ cup crushed corn flakes

1½ Tbsp. melted butter or oil

Instructions

1. Preheat oven to 350 degrees. Combine all ingredients into a greased 8×8 baking dish.

2. Mix up all the ingredients except corn flakes and butter or oil right in the baking dish.

3. Sprinkle the crushed corn flakes over the top of the casserole.

4. Drizzle melted butter or oil over the top.

5. Bake for 30–35 minutes or until casserole is heated through.

27. CHIPOTLE TORTILLA SOUP

PREP 10 MIN   COOK 4 HOURS

1 large onion, chopped (or ½ cup dehydrated onions)

4 garlic cloves, minced

4 cups chicken broth

2 (15-ounce) cans pinto beans or black beans, rinsed and drained

2 (14½-ounce) cans fire-roasted diced tomatoes, undrained

2 (15-ounce) cans corn,

2 chipotle peppers in adobo sauce from 1 (7-ounce) can, seeded and minced

2 tsp. adobo sauce (the sauce comes with the chipotle peppers)

1 tsp. ground cumin

¼ tsp. pepper

2 (12-ounce) cans (or 2 pints chicken) (optional: drain and use liquid towards the needed broth)

¼ cup minced fresh cilantro (or 2 Tbsp. dried cilantro)

Instructions

1. In a slow cooker add garlic, onions, broth, beans, tomatoes, corn, chipotle peppers, adobo sauce, chicken, cumin, and pepper. Cook on low 8 hours or high 4 hours.

28. GARLIC POTATO SOUP

PREP 10 MIN   COOK 20 MIN

3½ cups chicken broth

4 cloves garlic, minced

4 cups potatoes, cubed (or 2 cups dehydrated potatoes + 1 cup water)

1 cup carrots, diced (or ½ cup dehydrated carrot + ½ cup water)

½ cup onion, chopped (or ¼ cup dehydrated onion + 2 Tbsp. water)

½ cup celery, chopped (or ¼ cup dehydrated or ½ cup freeze-dried celery + 2 Tbsp. water)

2 slices bacon, cooked and crumbled, optional

1 cup milk (or 3 Tbsp. dry milk powder + 1 cup water)

1 cup potato flakes or pearls

1 tablespoon chopped fresh parsley

Instructions

1. Heat the broth, garlic, potatoes, carrots, onion, celery and bacon in a 4-quart saucepan over medium-high heat to a boil. Reduce the heat to low. Cover and cook for 15 minutes or until the vegetables are tender.

2. Reduce the heat to medium. Stir the milk, potato flakes and parsley in the saucepan. Cook until the mixture is hot and bubbling, stirring occasionally.

Dessert

2

3

Let's face it, dessert is comfort food and in times of stress it may just be the perfect thing to make your life, well sweeter. While dessert every night is probably not realistic, you can at least plan on it once a week as a special treat.

GET OUR BEST TIPS FOR ADDING WHEAT FLOUR TO YOUR FAVORITE BAKED GOODS ON PAGE 135

4

5

6

7

1. No-Fail Chocolate Cake – pg. 132
This decadent cake is the easiest chocolate cake you'll ever make.

2. Low-fat Oatmeal Raisin Cookies – pg. 132
Learn how to use beans to make these deliciously moist cookies low-fat.

3. Food Storage Ice Cream – pg. 132
You'll never want freeze-dried ice cream when you can have the real thing!

4. Coconut Macaroons – pg. 132
Learn how to make your own sweetened condensed milk from your powdered milk!

5. Brownies – pg. 133
Whole-wheat is perfect in this chocolatey treat.

6. Nutella Braid Bread – pg. 133
Use your favorite chocolate hazelnut spread to make this delectable dessert.

7. Angel Food Cake – pg. 133
Simply delicious, it will satisfy any craving.

1. NO-FAIL CHOCOLATE CAKE

PREP 10 MIN BAKE 35 MIN

2 cups sugar

1¾ cups flour (whole wheat is fine)

¾ cup cocoa or dark cocoa

1½ tsp. baking powder

1½ tsp. baking soda

1 tsp. salt

2 eggs (or ¼ cup dry egg powder + ½ cup water)

1 cup milk (or 3 Tbsp. non-instant dry milk powder + 1 cup water)

½ cup oil (or bean purée)

2 Tbsp. vanilla

1 cup boiling water

Instructions

1. Heat oven to 375. Spray 9-inch round pans, 13×9 or bundt baking pan.

2. Beat all ingredients except boiling water on medium speed of electric mixer 2 minutes. Stir in boiling water (batter will be thin). Pour batter into prepared pans.

3. Bake 30–35 minutes for round pans, 35–40 minutes for 9×13 pan or 50–55 minutes for bundt pan or until toothpick inserted in center comes out clean. Cool 10 minutes and remove from pans to wire racks.

CHOCOLATE GLAZE

3 Tbsp. cocoa

2 Tbsp butter flavored shortening, melted

1 cup powdered sugar

3 Tbsp. warm water

½ tsp. vanilla

Instructions

1. Melt your shortening. Add all other ingredients.

2. Stir until well mixed and smooth.

3. Add more water if you want it thinner at this point. If using as icing and you think it's too thick just let it sit for a few minutes.

2. LOW-FAT OATMEAL RAISIN COOKIES

PREP 15 MIN BAKE 8–10 MIN

1 cup shortening (or 1 cup white beans)

1 cup brown sugar (or 1 cup white sugar + 2 Tbsp. molasses)

1 cup white sugar

2 eggs (or 2 Tbsp. dry powdered eggs + ¼ cup water)

1 tsp. vanilla

1½ cup wheat flour

1 tsp. salt

1 tsp. soda

3 cups oats

2 tsp. cinnamon

2 cups raisins

Instructions

1. Cream together shortening (or beans), sugars, eggs, and vanilla.

2. Combine dry ingredients and mix into wet ingredients.

3. Stir in raisins.

4. Drop by rounded tablespoonfuls and bake for 8–10 minutes at 375 degrees.

Hint: Soak the raisins in water with the 1 tsp. vanilla called for in the recipe. This will make the raisins plump and juicy; plus, they will taste like vanilla. If you don't have a lot of time you can heat the water, vanilla, and raisins in the microwave for 2 minutes. Remember that you can definitely use your leftover water to hydrate your food storage powdered eggs!

3. Food Storage Ice Cream

PREP 10 MIN FREEZE 1–2 HOURS

4 eggs (or 4 Tbsp. dry egg powder + ½ cup water*)

2½ cups sugar

2 Tbsp. vanilla

½ tsp. salt

6 cups milk

4 cups evaporated milk

Instructions

1. Using wire whisk, beat together eggs and sugar until light and creamy. Whisk in vanilla and salt, then slowly add in milks. Mix until thoroughly combined, about 1 minute Pour mixture into in 4 quart ice cream maker container, and then freeze as per your ice cream maker instructions. Freezing takes about 60 minutes.

For less "egg" flavor use the OvaEasy Egg Crystals instead of the egg powder.

4. Coconut Macaroons

PREP 15 MIN BAKE 12–15 MIN

⅔ cups flour

5½ cups flaked coconut

¼ tsp. salt

1 (14-ounce) can sweetened condensed milk or make from powder milk

2 tsp. vanilla extract

Instructions

1. Preheat oven to 350 degrees F. Line cookie sheets with parchment paper or aluminum foil.
2. In a large bowl, stir together the flour, coconut and salt. Stir in the sweetened condensed milk and vanilla using your hands until well blended. Use an ice cream scoop to drop dough onto the prepared cookie sheets. Cookies should be about golf-ball size.
3. Bake for 12 to 15 minutes in the preheated oven, until coconut is toasted.

5. BROWNIES

PREP 10 MIN BAKE 20–25 MIN

½ cup vegetable oil (or ½ cup bean purée; instructions found on page 52)

1 cup white sugar

1 tsp. vanilla extract

2 eggs (or 2 Tbsp. dry egg powder + ¼ cup water)

½ cup flour

⅓ cup unsweetened cocoa powder

¼ tsp. baking powder

¼ tsp. salt

½ cup chopped nuts, if desired

Instructions

1. Preheat oven to 350 degrees F Grease a 9×9 inch baking pan.
2. In a medium bowl, mix together the oil (or bean purée), sugar, and vanilla. Beat in eggs. Combine flour, cocoa, baking powder, and salt; gradually stir into the egg mixture until well blended. Stir in walnuts, if desired. Spread the batter evenly into the prepared pan.
3. Bake for 20 to 25 minutes, or until the brownie begins to pull away from edges of pan. Let cool on a wire rack before cutting into squares.

6. Nutella Braid Bread

PREP 1 HOUR BAKE 20–25 MIN

2¼ tsp. yeast

½ cup milk (1 ½ Tbsp. dry milk powder + ½ cup water)

¼ cup sugar

½ cup warm water

1 tsp. salt

3 Tbsp. oil

3½ cups flour

about 1 cup of Nutella

Instructions

1. In a small bowl, add the water, yeast and 1 tsp of the sugar. Set aside for 5 minutes.

2. In the bowl of a standing mixer fitted with a dough hook, mix together the flour, remaining sugar and salt.
3. Add the oil, milk (unless you are using powdered milk, add the dry powder last after the flour to prevent clumping) and yeast mixture, mix it until it comes together, then with the speed on medium, let it knead for about 7 minutes or until you have a smooth dough.
4. Place the dough into an oiled bowl, cover with plastic wrap and place it a warm spot to rise and double in volume, about an hour.
5. Roll out dough to a 10"×15" rectangle, smear the surface with some Nutella, and roll it tightly like a jelly roll, starting from one of the longer sides.
6. Cut the loaf in half lengthwise (the inside will be exposed) and roll it in a two strand braid making sure to pinch the top and bottom ends to seal it; place it on a parchment paper–lined baking sheet.
7. Cover loosely with a kitchen towel and place them somewhere warm to rest for about half an hour, meanwhile, preheat your oven to 350 degrees.
8. Bake the bread for about 20 to 25 minutes or until golden brown all around, allow to cool, and dig in!!

7. Angel Food Cake

PREP 30 MIN BAKE 30–35 MIN

1½ cup powdered sugar

1 cup cake flour (or ¾ cup whole wheat flour + ¼ cup cornstarch)

1½ cup egg whites (or ½ cup dry egg white powder + 1½ cup water)

1½ tsp. cream of tartar

1 cup. granulated sugar

2 tsp. vanilla

¼ tsp. salt

Instructions

1. Move oven rack to lowest position. Heat oven to 375ºF.
2. Pulse in blender powdered sugar and flour; set aside. Beat egg whites and cream of tartar in large bowl with electric mixer on medium speed until foamy. Beat in granulated sugar, 2 tablespoons at a time, on high speed, adding vanilla, and salt with the last addition of sugar. Continue beating until stiff and glossy meringue forms. Do not under beat.
3. Sprinkle sugar-flour mixture, ¼ cup at a time, over meringue, folding in just until sugar-flour mixture disappears. Push batter into ungreased angel food cake pan (tube pan), 10×4 inches. Cut gently through batter with metal spatula.
4. Bake 30 to 35 minutes or until cracks feel dry and top springs back when touched lightly. Immediately turn pan upside down onto heatproof funnel or bottle. Let hang about 2 hours or until cake is completely cool. Loosen side of cake with knife or long metal spatula; remove from pan.

See page 134 for *Raspberry Syrup* recipe

Homemade Noodles

1 egg, beaten (or 1 Tbsp. dry egg powder + 2 Tbsp. water)

½ tsp. salt

1 cup flour

2 Tbsp. water

Instructions

1. In a medium sized bowl, combine flour and salt. Make a well in the flour, add the slightly beaten egg, and mix. Mixture should form a stiff dough. If needed, stir in 1 to 2 tablespoons water.

2. On a lightly floured surface, knead dough for about 3 to 4 minutes. With a pasta machine or by hand roll dough out to desired thinness. Use machine or knife to cut into strips of desired width.

Raspberry Syrup

1½ cups freeze-dried raspberries

2 cups water

½ cup sugar

1 Tbsp. lemon juice

Instructions

1. Blend ingredients in blender. If you want it warm, make sure to transfer it to a microwave safe container and heat until warmed through.

Pan Tip: We've learned an important lesson when it comes to Angel Food Cake: the pan matters! Most angel food cake pans sold at stores like Walmart are only 9⅜ inches tall, and if you bake a cake that rises too high, you may be disappointed, because it will fall when you flip it over. We highly suggest investing in a 10 inch Angel Food Cake pan.

Making Sweetened Condensed Milk from Powdered Milk

½ cup hot water

1 cup dry milk powder

1 cup sugar

1 Tbsp. butter, optional (or 1 Tbsp. butter powder)

Instructions

1. Blend in blender very well. Can be stored in the refrigerator or frozen. Use in place of one can of sweetened condensed milk.

Making Evaporated Milk from Powdered Milk

1½ cups water

½ cup + 1 Tbsp. dry milk powder

Instructions

1. Combine ingredients and add to your recipe. Or add dry milk powder to dry ingredients and water to wet ingredients and follow recipe as instructed.

OUR BEST TIPS FOR BAKING WITH
Wheat Flour

SHOULD I USE RED OR WHITE WHEAT?

Red wheat has a stronger, nuttier flavor. The white wheat has a more delicate flavor that is much easier to disguise. So we would suggest always using the white wheat-especially in baked goods. Red wheat IS more nutritious—and by more nutritious, we mean that it has 2% more protein than the white—HOWEVER, in order to make most anything palatable with 100% red wheat you have to mix it half and half with the all-purpose flour. In that case, you've just cut the nutrition by half….or you could just use the 2% less protein white wheat flour and use it 100%. Now, do you think we mean that you ALWAYS have to use 100% wheat in your baking? NO! You use it how your family would like it, and we'll give you some good tips for how to use it successfully and how to know if your recipe is best for 100% whole wheat, half and half, or less.

SUBSTITUTING FOR 100% WHOLE WHEAT

There are a lot of recipes that are great for substituting 100% whole wheat flour. We'd say as a general rule of thumb, if your recipe has two or more of the following ingredients in it-you're good to go with 100% whole wheat.

- At least equal amounts of brown sugar and white sugar. All brown sugar or more brown sugar than white sugar works even better!
- Strong spices like cinnamon, cloves, nutmeg, pumpkin pie spice, apple pie spice, etc.
- Mashed fruit (non-citrus) or vegetables like bananas, zucchini, pumpkin, etc.
- Nuts. Wheat is very complimentary to nuts.
- Oats. Oats already have that hearty feeling and wheat goes great with it!
- Chocolate. Let's be honest, chocolate covers a myriad of flavors and tastes great!

USING HALF WHOLE WHEAT AND HALF ALL-PURPOSE FLOUR IN YOUR RECIPES

So what to do if you recipe doesn't have two of the above? Think sugar cookies, white cake, etc. If you're at all nervous you can always do one-sixth wheat flour with LITTLE to NO taste difference. If you're feeling a little daring, you can do half whole wheat flour and half all-purpose. You may be able to taste the wheat a little but it doesn't mean it's a bad flavor. Remember, with cooking just because it tastes different doesn't automatically mean it tastes bad. It just means it tastes different and you if have to decide if you like it better or worse that way.

DIY GUIDE

Tools and Tips for Everyone Who Wants to Do It Themselves

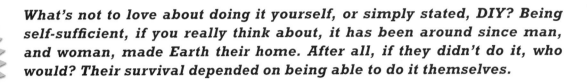

BONUS CHAPTER

What's not to love about doing it yourself, or simply stated, DIY? Being self-sufficient, if you really think about, it has been around since man, and woman, made Earth their home. After all, if they didn't do it, who would? Their survival depended on being able to do it themselves.

WHY do-it-yourself?

For early settlers, gathering, growing, and figuring out a way to preserve their food for times when they couldn't find any determined not only how well they ate, but if they ate at all. Years later, those who were the best at farming, raising chickens, weaving, or baking opened their own businesses, where people traded their goods for things that they needed. But it really wasn't until fairly recently that society as a whole became almost completely dependent on others for all our human needs.

Think about it—we purchase from others most everything that we need for basic survival. Most of us don't grow or raise our own food, go out to our well to get a bucket of water, or sew our own clothes. Now, don't misunderstand us, we love our modern conveniences as much as you do. But when you think about it, we are just one natural disaster or truck strike away from empty supermarket shelves. That is why storing food is so important. But let's be honest, it can be downright expensive especially if you want variety, nutrition and the ease of mixes in your home storage. This is why it is so important to have DIY skills.

Learning and honing DIY skills is so easy right now. There is truly a DIY movement across the country and throughout the world. People like yourselves are learning new skills and sharing them on social media so others can learn from their triumphs and boo-boos.

Now is the time for you to join the movement. Read through our DIY chapter. Find one that interests you, gather the supplies you need, and just start doing it. Even better, find a friend or two and do it together. We promise you will LOVE it! Having a backyard garden is a peaceful place to unwind after a hard day, and then there is the added benefit of being able to pick and eat fresh food from that garden. Even more satisfying is being able to go to your cupboard in the cold winter months and take out a jar of beautiful, bright peaches that you preserved during the summer. Yum! Learning these skills will not only help you save money but they are one of the best ways for you to truly feel self-reliant.

There are many skills that would be handy to have, but we are going to touch on these:

- Gardening
- Dehydrating
- Canning
- Sprouting

GARDEN know-how

TOOLS AND TIPS FOR EVERYONE WHO WANTS TO LOVE DIGGING

GARDENING: YOUR OTHER FOOD STORAGE

Planting a garden, even a small one, allows for a greater degree of self-reliance. With careful attention to factors such as seed selection, planting times, soil preparation and fertilization, and watering, anyone from a first-time gardener to an experienced "green thumb" can cultivate a productive garden.

WHY GARDEN?

1 One of the important keys of gardening is the acquisition of skills. We may be able to buy food easily now, but the skills and intuitive wisdom gained through gardening are worth more than the time and effort they require. In a sustained emergency, basic gardening know-how is invaluable.

2 Gardening teaches kids the value of hard work and a natural love for fruits and vegetables. Give kids simple tasks to do and they will enjoy spending time both with the family and in the garden. Most kids love to help. Even younger kids can pick vegetables, water plants, or pull weeds with a little bit of guidance. Chances are they won't even view it as work, but they'll be learning the value of hard work, responsibility, and how to follow directions, all the while spending quality time with the family.

3 Gardening not only promotes good health from the inside by nourishing your body with good food, but it's also great exercise that helps to keep you both physically and mentally fit. In addition to increasing your flexibility and helping to improve muscle tone, by spending time outdoors you will also benefit from getting vitamin D naturally. A backyard garden can be a peaceful place to unwind after a hard day, helping to reduce stress and clear and recharge your mind.

We love Mel Bartholomew's book and highly suggest adding it to your collection. It has revolutionized gardening.

SQUARE FOOT GARDENING

The easiest, weed-free, perfect soil, organic way to garden for beginners and advanced alike. In just six easy steps you can have a thriving garden.

I. THE RAISED GARDEN BED: Purchase or build garden boxes. There are many different options for purchasing a raised garden bed, from cedar wood to plastic. Pick your best option depending on where you live and your budget. Or there are many free plans for building your own raised bed garden. It can be as easy as putting old wood together in a square or even lining up concrete blocks.

2. THE SOIL: Lucky you! The perfect raised garden bed soil is sold at most Home Depots nationwide (even if it isn't sold at your local Home Depot, it is sold on their website). It's called Mel's Mix (named after Mel Bartholomew, the father of Square Foot Gardening). It may be a little more expensive than other soil varieties, but it is a lot cheaper and faster than cultivating your backyard soil (which can take up to 7 years) or driving all over town to find the right ingredients to make your own soil blend.

3. THE GRID: On top of each raised garden bed you will need a permanent grid that divides the box into one foot squares. The grid is the unique feature that makes the whole system work so well. Grids can be made from nearly any material; wood, plastic strips, old venetian blinds, etc., or even purchased on Amazon. The grid can be cut long enough to fit across the top of the box or cut shorter to lay on the soil inside the box.

4. PLANT: Plant one or two seeds in each spot by making a shallow hole with your finger. Cover, but do not pack the soil. Thinning is all but eliminated. Seeds are not wasted. Extra seeds can be stored cool and dry in your refrigerator. Don't over-plant. Plant only as much of any one crop as you will use. This 4 foot by 4 foot box will grow more than a conventional garden that is 8 foot by 10 foot.

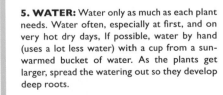

5. WATER: Water only as much as each plant needs. Water often, especially at first, and on very hot dry days, If possible, water by hand (uses a lot less water) with a cup from a sun-warmed bucket of water. As the plants get larger, spread the watering out so they develop deep roots.

6. HARVEST: Harvest continually, and when a crop in one square is gone, add some new compost and plant a new different crop in that square.

DRY it, you'll like it!

TOOLS AND TIPS FOR EVERYONE WHO WANTS TO START DEHYDRATING

DEHYDRATING: DIY FOOD STORAGE

People have been drying food for thousands of years. In the beginning, the sun and air were used to dry out their grain and fruits for the long winter months when no fresh fruits and vegetables were available. Dehydrating removes moisture from food so bacteria, yeasts, & molds can't grow and spoil food.

WHICH DEHYDRATOR IS BEST FOR YOU?

1 👎 **INEXPENSIVE DEHYDRATOR:**
Don't be tempted by inexpensive dehydrators! We have both made that mistake, and all it did was make us not want to dehydrate. They definitely don't dry evenly and produce a subpar product. If you'd like to experiment before committing to a purchase, ask around; chances are someone has a dehydrator you can borrow.

2 👍 **L'EQUIP DEHYDRATOR:** $120, *Amazon.com*

Six stacking trays for a total of 12 square feet of drying space

Three different temperature settings

Efficient side fan dehydrates evenly.

The complete drying guide, plus 398 recipes and instructions foe making jerky.

THE ULTIMATE
DEHYDRATOR COOKBOOK

3 👍 **EXCALIBUR DEHYDRATOR:** $226, *Amazon.com*

Built in on/off switch and adjustable thermostat with 26 hour timer.

9-Tray dehydrator, 15 square feet of drying space.

Includes a flexible polyscreen tray insert to prevent foods from sticking

Efficient side fan dehydrates evenly.

DEHYDRATING BASICS

Why dehydrate? Well, there are four easy reasons: 1) It's a quick and easy way to preserve food; 2) it saves money to buy on sale and dry; 3) dried food takes up much less space than fresh or canned food; and 4) it is a great way to add variety to your family's long-term food storage. Below are the necessary steps to begin dehydrating, be sure to always consult your dehydrator's manual for specific instructions.

WHICH FOODS TO DRY?

The best quality dried foods begin with the best quality foods available. Fruits and vegetables to be dried should be picked or bought at their peak of flavor and freshness.

THE EASY WAY TO DEHYDRATE

Frozen Food: You can also dehydrate all your frozen fruits and vegetables from your grocery store, saving room in your freezer and tons of time! All your frozen foods have already been prepped, just open the bag and throw them on the tray frozen. This includes thick French fries and hash browns.

How to prepare fruits & veggies?

To prepare vegetables you will need to wash, core, trim, and peel, and, if necessary, slice or chop. Remember that the food will shrink when drying, so chop the pieces large enough that they won't fall through the racks. To prepare fruits, wash fruit and core, if needed.

Fruits can be halved or sliced (apples, bananas, citrus) and some left whole. If fruit is dried whole, "check" or crack the skin to speed drying; cranberries—place in boiling then cold water to "check."

How do I pre-treat the fruit & vegetables?

Pre-treating, or blanching, is necessary for most vegetables (not: peppers, collard greens, spinach, mushrooms, onions, or garlic) to keep them from turning brown, black or rotting during storage. Some fruits have a better texture when dehydrated if blanched first. These include: apricots, blueberries, cranberries, gooseberries, currants, grapes (raisins), peaches, and plums (prunes).

Blanching: Fill a large pan over half-full with water. Bring the water to a boil and stir the food directly into the boiling water. Start counting time as soon as water returns to boil. If it takes more than 1 minute to return to boil, you are putting in too many vegetables at a time. Blanch for about 3 minutes. Remove food into ice water for a few minutes to cool, drain and blot with a towel to remove excess water before drying.

How to know if it's done?

Dehydrator temperatures should not go above 120°. Double check your dehydrator's instructions for more details.

- Dry vegetables until brittle or crisp (Root vegetables, squash and pumpkin will be tough and leathery but still pliable.

- Check dried vegetables for moisture once or twice for the first couple of weeks.

How to Tell if Fruit is Done

- Let food cool 5–10 minutes before testing.

- Cut several cooled pieces in half there should be no visible moisture and you should not be able to squeeze any moisture from fruit

- Should not be sticky or tacky, should spring back when squeezed together.

- If folded in half, it shouldn't stick to itself.

- Peaches, pears, apples and plums should remain pliable but others such as berries should be crisp. Banana chips can be either.

How to store it?

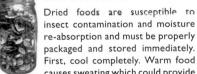

Dried foods are susceptible to insect contamination and moisture re-absorption and must be properly packaged and stored immediately. First, cool completely. Warm food causes sweating which could provide enough moisture for mold to grow. Pack foods into clean, dry insect-proof containers as tightly as possible without crushing. If you are going to use your dried foods within a month or two, you can just put them into Ziplocs or Tupperware-type containers.

- Store dried foods in clean, dry home canning jars, plastic freezer containers with tight-fitting lids or in plastic freezer bags.

- Vacuum packaging using Food Saver or Seal-a-Meal is also a good option.

- Pack foods in amounts that can be used all at once. Each time a package is re-opened, the food is exposed to air and moisture that can lower the quality of the food and result in spoilage.

The taste and quality of all stored food is affected by HALT: *humidity, air, light, and temperature.* The drier; less oxygen; darker and cooler it is the longer the food will taste good. Food quality is affected mostly by heat. For instance, if the food is stored at a constant temperature of 60°, it will store for 20 years; if stored at 95° it will last 2.5 years. Cooler is much better. If you are going to store things in the Mylar or food saver bags you will need to put them in buckets with gamma lids to keep the rodents and light out.

Oxygen packs are small oxygen absorbing packages that are to be placed into your vacuum sealed bags, buckets, or cans of dehydrated foods. The purpose of an oxygen pack is to absorb any residual oxygen that might be present in your bag or can, allowing your food to store much longer.

you CAN do it!

TOOLS AND TIPS FOR EVERYONE WHO WANTS TO START CANNING

HOME CANNING MADE EASY!

DIY canning is a great way to preserve produce from your garden into jams and jellies or bite sized fruits and vegetables. If you want to really save money, then do some quick and easy canning with beans, meat or even meals. Home-canned foods taste better and store longer than foods in metal cans. It also allows you to customize your product to fit your family's wants and needs. There are two different kinds of canning: water bath or pressure canning. No matter which of these methods you use, there are some easy steps that apply to all of them.

CANNING RULES MADE SIMPLE

- Keep it clean
- Have the proper tools: canner, utensils, timer
- Sanitize jars and lids
- Prepare canner
- Prepare food products
- Pack jars to appropriate level; add liquid if needed
- Remove air bubbles, if needed
- Wipe and close jars
- Load canner
- Process and set timer
- When done processing, unload canner
- Cool jars 12–24 hours
- Test jars for proper seal
- Remove rings; wash outside of jars
- Label and date
- Store jars in cool, dark place

WHAT IS YOUR ALTITUDE?

When canning, how far you live above sea level is very important in determining how long and at what pressure you processes the jars. Don't know your altitude? Find it at

http://nchfp.uga.edu/how/can_home.html

Then click to find your elevation.

Always consult a good, up-to-date canning book or reputable canning website for specific canning instructions and guidelines.

THE RIGHT CANNING TOOLS

Having the best tools for the job can make all the difference whether or not you will have an enjoyable and successful experience or a frustrating canning experience. Here's our list of the best tools to invest in and some you shouldn't waste your money on.

Funnel, Magnetic Lid Lifter, & Jar Lifter: Having the right tools can make any job easier. A good funnel will keep you from spilling and make less mess. The magnetic lid lifter will save your finger tips from the steaming water you will soak the lids in before canning and keep everything sanitary. The jar lifter is mandatory for removing the jars from the canner.

WATER BATH CANNER: This is used for high-acid foods, such as jams, jellies, and most fruit. They are usually made from black ceramic on steel or aluminum and hold up to seven quart jars. A canner basket, which is used to keep the jars off the bottom and makes it easy to raise and lower jars, is usually included. Water bath canners are inexpensive, about $25 and can be purchased online or where canning supplies are sold.

We love the All-American pressure canner

PRESSURE CANNER is used for canning vegetables, beans, meats, and meals. Modern pressure canners are very safe and made of aluminum or stainless steel. They include a bottom rack and sometimes extra racks to double or even triple layer your jars; a steam vent, and a safety vent.

Warning: Pressure canner companies do not recommend their usage on glass stovetops since the high heat can crack the glass. They also do not recommend using a high heat camping stove as this can warp your canner.

A GOOD pressure canner has:
• Weighted or Pop-up Pressure Indicator
• Usually made from lightweight aluminum making them easy to lift.
• A lock in place lid; a pressure indicator gauge and a safety valve.
• Has a rubber gasket that needs to be replaced every few years.
• Cost about $70.

The BEST Pressure Canner:
• Made of heavy cast aluminum and is built to last generations, has no rubber gasket.
• It has a dial gauge (to see the pressure), a weighted gauge, and a safety valve.
• Weighted gauge makes rattling sound to let you know it is keeping the correct pressure.
• Comes in a variety of sizes, from 7 pint or 4 quart jars up to 39 pints or 19 quarts.
• Costs range from $190-$455.

Dial Gauge Only Pressure Canner: Dial gauges need to be recalibrated each year to be sure they are functioning properly (a big pain); they need to be watched constantly during processing to be sure the pressure doesn't drop (a waste of time); they have rubber gaskets that need to be replaced.

Bottles, Lids & Rings: Bottles should be well-tested brands like Kerr or Ball brand bottles. Lids should also be good brands like Kerr or Ball and be unused (the jury is still out on re-usable lids and their safety). Using the right bottles and lids will ensure a better seal. Rings can be used over and over again but jars shouldn't be stored with the rings on.

STEAM CANNER: Looks like an upside down water bath canner. It consists of a shallow pan, a fitted rack and a high domed cover. It is typically advertised as an alternative to the boiling water bath canner (it is not the same as a pressure canner). Currently, steam canners are not recommended for home use by either the USDA or the National Center for Home Food Preservation. Their reasoning is that steam isn't as effective at transmitting heat through to the center of the jars as boiling water is. It's this heat penetration that ensures both the safety of your product (it kills off any possible contaminants) and the effectiveness of your lid seal.

CANNING YOUR OWN
MEAT

If you really want to have meat as part of your food storage but can't afford the $12 per pound or more that freeze-dried meats cost, then step right up and join the ranks of do-it-yourself meat packers, aka canners. You won't believe how EASY it is to can meat. The price will depend on the type and price of meat you are canning and a canning jar with lid, but that's about it folks.

One pint-sized jar (wide mouth works best) holds about one pound of tender, cooked meat, ready to open and add to the meal of a family of four. One of the best parts of home canning is you can preserve almost any kind of meat, poultry, and even fish (warning: strong fish odor in house) that your family likes and at a great price!

You can bottle your own chicken for under $3 a pound.
THAT IS A WHOPPING 75% SAVINGS
over the freeze-dried variety!

COLD PACK MEAT CANNING:

The fastest and easiest way to can meat is to cold pack it. This simply means: pack raw meat in the jars. The cooking is done during the processing. This can be done in three easy steps:

1. Cut up the meat

2. Fill the jars

3. Process the meat

Doesn't that sound easy? Of course, you need to follow proper canning protocols found in your canning book and manual, but seriously, this is pretty much all there is to canning meat.

HOT PACK MEAT CANNING (cooking meat first and adding hot liquid into hot jars) is only recommended (by us) for hamburger and meat sauces. If you want to hot pack, refer to canning book for additional canning steps.

FOOD SAFETY TIP:

Meat properly processed—meaning at right pressure for your altitude; for right amount of time; with unbroken seal—will store safely for many, many years. For best taste rotate every 2–3 years. If concerned about botulism: boil 10 minutes, adding 1 minute for every 1000 feet above sea level.

CANNING YOUR OWN

BEANS

You might be asking yourself, "Why should I can beans when I can buy them at the store?" Honestly, many of us wonder this. The answer is simply . . . because we "can." We can take control of our own food storage destiny and beans are a great place to do it. Like meat, canning beans is super easy, and it gives you control over the ingredients and flavors.

Having home canned beans is a great addition to your everyday and 90-day food storage, but you know what is even better about canning beans? Having "bean canning skills," bean recipes that you love, and the right ingredients and equipment to Do-It-Yourself! You know what else is great about canning your own beans? Saving LOTS of money! For example, if you can your own beans at home using dry beans from a box store, grocery store or an LDS Home Store Center,

it's the equivalent of buying one 15-ounce can of beans and

GETTING SIX MORE FOR FREE!

You could buy a lot of food storage with those savings!

BEAN CANNING SIMPLIFIED:

1. Sort and rinse dry beans.

2. Soak beans 8–12 hours, drain, and rinse.

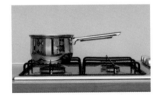

3. Cover beans with water; cook for 30 minutes.

4. Fill jars with beans (1½ inches from top); add water to bottom of rim.

5. Wipe rim; add lid and ring.

6. Process beans in pressure canner.

Be sure and consult a good canning book or official canning website to get the canning specifics for your jar size, altitude, and canner, and to try out some recipes.

WEB WARNING
There is a bean canning process making the rounds on the web, where you just clean and rinse beans, put them in a canning jar ¼ full of beans, fill with water, and process with no soaking. The Utah State Extension office says that because the beans are dry in the middle (no moisture when the processing starts), it creates a perfect opportunity for botulism growth. Soak your beans before canning them.

all about SPROUTS

TOOLS AND TIPS FOR EVERYONE WHO WANTS TO START SPROUTING

SPROUTING: YOUR INDOOR GARDEN

If you want to add variety and A LOT of nutrition to your food storage, all without having to get your hands dirty, then sprouting is for you! Sprouting is a simple process of soaking, rinsing and draining a variety of beans, grains and seeds which then transforms them into little healthy, live plants.

WHY SPROUT?

1 **SPROUTS AREN'T JUST FOR SALADS ANYMORE!** Gone are the days when sprouts are just eaten in salads. Now it is common to see fresh sprouts used in blended drinks and sprouted bread; in omelets, sandwiches, and wraps; in pancakes and hot cereal; and in soup, meatloaf, and other main dishes. All can benefit from eating sprouts, especially those who have a problem digesting grains. Try it; you just may be surprised how easy it is and how much you like growing and eating sprouts.

2 **SPROUTING AIDS IN DIGESTION:** Have you ever had problems with beans and legumes causing intestinal gas? Well, sprouting helps break down the complex sugars responsible for all of that gas, making them easier to digest. Also, soaking grains helps to break down the complex carbohydrates into simpler and easier-to-digest glucose molecules. And, finally, sprouting helps neutralize enzyme inhibitors, which helps you digest your food.

3 **NUTRITIONAL ADVANTAGES:** Sprouting increases the fiber and protein content as well as dramatically increasing the vitamin content, especially of A, B, C, E, and K. The vitamin content of some seeds, grains, or beans can increase up to 20 times the original value.

4 **SPROUTING MAKES HEALTHY EATING INEXPENSIVE:** People frequently use the cost of healthy food as an excuse for not eating healthy. But with sprouts being so cheap, there really is no excuse for not eating healthier.

SPROUTING BASICS

Are Sprouts Safe to Eat?

Over the past fifteen years you may have heard or read about *E. coli*, salmonella, or listeria outbreaks associated with eating alfalfa, radish, clover, or mung bean sprouts. All of these incidents involved contaminated seeds or were watered with contaminated water. There have been no reported cases of illness when using certified organic beans, grains, or seeds for sprouts and when washing and rinsing with clean water. There have been no reported illnesses when sprouts are used in heated or baked foods as heat kills the bacteria. If there is any doubt or concern, then children under the age of six, people older than 60, people with weak immune systems, or pregnant women should avoid eating sprouts.

SIMPLY SPROUTING: To sprout all you need is a jar, lid ring, piece of screen or cheesecloth, water, and something to sprout (beans, grains, seed).

Step 1: Rinse seeds.

Step 2: Soak seeds in water (1:3 ratio); 8–12 hours.

Step 3: Drain; rinse thoroughly; drain again.

Step 4: Leave jar on angle to continue to drain.

Step 5: Repeat steps 3 & 4, 2–3 times per day for 2–3 days

Step 6: Eat, cook, or store sprouts in refrigerator.

Sprouted Flour?

Is there a way to get the benefits without eating fresh sprouts? Yes, just sprout as usual, and then dry the sprouted grain at 150° oven or dehydrator and grind as usual in your grinder. Use this flour just as you normally would in baked goods, tortillas, or even gravy, but it will contain all the benefits of sprouts.

A final word

TOGETHER WE CAN MAKE A REAL DIFFERENCE

MAKE A COMMITMENT

You now know more about how to plan and begin a great long-term food supply than 90 percent of the people who will ever have or try to have a long-term food storage. In short, you are ready to get going. So, right now, make a commitment to yourself to make this happen. Our hunch is that in no time you'll have a fantastic long-term food supply by your side, saving you money, helping you eat healthier, and preparing you for any emergency that may come your way.

Having bought this book and read it all the way through to the end makes you very special. Many people buy books about food storage, but few ever actually finish them. So congratulations! We hope you have been inspired to take some simple actions that will have a dramatic impact on your life over the long term.

The principles you've learned over the course of reading this book are tried-and-true strategies for building a successful and USEFUL food storage plan. But don't just focus on the results. You deserve to enjoy the journey.

Having a successful and useful food storage plan and supply of food is not simply about accumulating food. It's also about relieving stress and worries about the future—about putting yourself in a place that enables you to enjoy life now as well as in the future. In other words, having a food storage plan should not only change your future, it should also change your present.

We hope you close this book inspired to make a successful plan for your food storage. Nothing helps you achieve success faster than helping others. Giving back to others will make the world a better, more gentle place. This is something we believe with all our hearts. As we see it, one of the greatest reasons to have a food storage is ultimately to be able to help others. We are put here to make the world a better place and so we encourage you to give back to neighbors, communities, and food banks. The more you give, the more comes back to you. It is the flow of abundance that brings us more joy, more love, and more meaning in our lives.

So please consider sharing what you've learned in this book with someone you love. If you want to buy a copy of this book for a friend, that's great—but please know that our goal isn't simply to sell more books. It's to share the message. And the best way we know to do that is for you to live what you learn and prove it works. Together, we can really make a difference.

index

SCAN TO VISIT

WWW.STORETHISNOTTHAT.COM